NORTHERN FARM

*Also by Henry Beston
in Large Print:*

The Outermost House

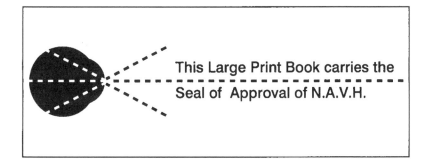

This Large Print Book carries the
Seal of Approval of N.A.V.H.

NORTHERN FARM

*A Glorious Year on a
Small Maine Farm*

HENRY BESTON

G.K. Hall & Co. • **Thorndike, Maine**

Published in 1999 by arrangement with Henry Holt & Company Inc.

G.K. Hall Large Print Perennial Bestseller Series.

The text of this Large Print edition is unabridged.
Other aspects of the book may vary from the original edition.

Set in 16 pt. Plantin by Rick Gundberg.

Printed in the United States on permanent paper.

Library of Congress Cataloging in Publication Data

Beston, Henry, 1888–1968.
  Northern farm: a glorious year on a small Maine farm / Henry Beston
    p.   cm.
    ISBN 0-7838-8657-8 (lg. print : hc : alk. paper)
    1. Beston, Henry, 1888–1968 — Homes and haunts — Maine.
2. Lincoln County (Me.) — Social life and customs. 3. Authors,
American — 20th century Biography. 4. Farmers — Maine —
Lincoln County Biography. 5. Farm life — Maine — Lincoln
County. 6. Large type books. I. Title.
    [PS3503.E784Z467 1999]
    630'.1—dc21   99-28762

TO
ROSALIND RICHARDS

FOREWORD

Our Maine year is no halfway affair. When it is summer, it is green summer at its best, and when the northern winter deepens out of October's brilliance and wholesome cold, it is the old-fashioned winter with its fields of snow, its sense of wintry peace, and its splendor of blue sky. I have tried in these pages to give an account of the adventure of living as a countryman sees it who lives in the farm country between the wide Kennebec and the Penobscot, on fresh water, yet only a little inland from the sea.

To his ever thoughtful and generous friends, Editor Morris H. Rubin of *The Progressive* and Associate Editor Mary Sheridan, the author wishes to make grateful acknowledgment of a first and outstanding debt. He began these "Country Chronicles" of Maine at their suggestion; their counsel and unfailing encouragement were ever at his service, and he now owes them thanks for permission to publish this present arrangement of his work. Were he to list the Maine friends and neighbors who have helped him on his way, the roll would be almost without end. Many of their names will be found in these pages, but he wishes to make particular mention of Henry Richards Esq. of Gardiner and the other kindest friends at the Yellow House above the Kennebec.

To the "Elizabeth" of these pages, my wife Elizabeth Coatsworth Beston, I would offer an acknowledgment which cannot quite be set down in words.

But I hear the farm-bell ringing; someone is at the door, so putting down pencil and paper, I leave these pages to the reader.

HENRY BESTON

Chimney Farm
Lincoln County
State of Maine

I

The train gathered speed, and from the red plush of the day coach, I watched the city withdraw to the south, and the immense slaty-black and brownish pall of smoke thin to a brownish veil over the suburbs and the dirty snow. Houses and open spaces which were neither country nor town slid fugitively by through the winter morning, together with local wildernesses of gravel and weedy birch, and then, after a crossing and a crossing bell, came a first sight of the true snowcovered country and a barn with patterns of snow upon the roof. My own land of the deeper snowfalls and the great evergreen woods was still close upon two hundred miles away, but the train was making good time, and the morning sun had cleared the cloud bank to the east. Home. Going home.

Something over a month had passed since I had seen the red farmhouse, the winter sky of the higher north, and the frozen pond with its wavering paths of ice and snow. At Christmas we had gone up the coast to spend the holidays near kinsmen outside the city, and somehow or other a hundred things to be attended to had lengthened our stay beyond the usual time. For several weeks our life had been the life of the suburb

9

with its old friends, its visits, and its welcomes, and now and then Elizabeth and I had gone to town. In spite of all the kindness and the good times, however, I had more than ever in my life felt unutterably homesick and uprooted. Home. Going home.

What had gone out of American life as one sees it in the city and the suburb? Essentially, thought I, musing by the window, a sense of direction. To use a metaphor, we were all of us passengers on a great ocean liner. There is plenty of food aboard, meals are served at given hours, and all goes on much the same as ever in the usual haphazard and familiar way. On the bridge there are quarrels as to who shall steer, and powerful and secret currents seize upon the keel. The pleasant-enough days go by; people read novels in sheltered corners of the deck. The ocean, however, is unknown, and no one, not a single soul, knows whither the ship is bound. Home. Going home.

Save for shelves of salt ice along its banks, the blue Kennebec was as open as any river below New York. Once across the great bridge, I scarce for a moment stopped looking out into the wooded distances, the austere air, and the increasingly brilliant day. My own country was beginning with its views down narrowing backwaters roofed with salt ice sagging with an outgoing tide and its distant glimpses of white steeple tops rising into the shining sky above the pines and snow. In one secluded cove in the woods, three black ducks had risen from a pool of open water and were flying away from the noise and roar of the train. Home. Going home.

And presently there I was, and in such a crystal splendor of light and under such a sun as I had not seen since I left the farm. A deep fall of snow about a fortnight old, having first been drenched with a mild rain, had then frozen over again with a smooth and solid crust of ice: from the pasture pines to the bounds of the horizon the entire landscape might have been dipped in a shining sea of arctic glass. Smoke rose from farm chimneys into the still air between the blue radiance above and the floors of ice, and there at a turn were the welcoming hands of my neighbors, the Olivers, and nearer the farm, the warm welcomes of Carroll and Louise, and Elaine telling me about her three months old Drusilla. How well they all looked and how cheerful, and what a pleasure it was to be hearing the neighborhood news and answering questions about Elizabeth. Home. Going home.

Above the ice of the pond, and the gleam of ice and light upon the slopes, the red farm seemed particularly serene. When I opened the door, the rooms were full of sunlight, quiet, and a sense of emptiness, yet they were welcoming too, for Carroll had with neighborly kindness kindled fires in the stoves. So still it was that all I could hear was the occasional tiny crack and twiglike snap of the coal fire. Then with a swing of the finger, I started the pendulum of the clock, and

11

with the steady tick, the life of the house began to beat. Home again. Home.

FARM DIARY

At Carroll and Louise Winchenbaugh's, the antlered head of one of last year's deer looks with unseeing glance from a rafter of the older barn whilst just below in a corner pen there studies me a young, genial, and trustful pig. / Monday, and a wool washing in the farm washtubs, and the steam of wool in the kitchens and heavy wools sagging and drying on the lines. / A sudden turn of the wind to the southwest blows in a drifting mass of seafog; the warm billows and tatters of vapor pass low over the fields and plains of ice, and, at night vast flares of lightning shake our wintry and northern world. / The closed-off rooms of the farm are just so many ice boxes, and when the full moon rises over the pond, the frost-covered windows on that side of the house become moonlit splendors from another age of time. / Snow flurries from the northwest, and a flight of snowbirds rises from the wet ground and uncovered grass about the flowing spring. / Welcome letters from Elizabeth saying to expect her on the Friday morning train.

As I settle down in this familiar house, with the

12

lamplight glowing from its windows and the great planets crossing the sky above its chimney tops, I find I am shaking off the strange oppression which came over me when I lived by an urban sense and understanding of time. In a world so convenient and artificial that there is scarcely day or night, and one is bulwarked against the seasons and the year, time, so to speak, having no natural landmarks, tends to stand still. The consequence is that life and time and history become unnaturally a part of some endless and unnatural present, and violence becomes for some the only remedy. Here in the country, it all moves ahead again. Spring is not only a landmark, but it looks ahead to autumn, and winter forever looks forward to the spring.

II

Our house stands above a pond, a rolling slope of old fields leading down to the tumble and jumble of rocks which make the shore. We do not see the whole pond but only a kind of comfortable bay some two miles long and perhaps a mile or so across. To the south lies a country road, a wooded vale, and a great farm above on a hill; across and to the east are woods again and then a more rural scene of farms and open land. It is the north, and as I set down these words the whole country lies quiescent in the cup of winter's hand.

Last night, coming in from the barn, I stood awhile in the moonlight looking down towards the pond in winter solitude. Because this year winds have swept the surface clean of early snows, the light of the high and wintry moon glowed palely upwards again from a sombre, even a black fixity of ice. Nothing could have seemed more frozen to stone, more a part of universal silence.

All about me, too, seemed still, field and faraway stand of pine lying frozen in the motionless air to the same moonlit absence of all sound. Had I paused but a moment and then closed the door behind me, I probably would have spoken of the silence of the night. But I lingered a long-ish while, and lingering found that the seeming stillness was but the interval between the shuddering, the mysterious outcrying of the frozen pond. For the pond was hollow with sound, as it is sometimes when the nights are bitter and the ice is free from snow.

It is the voice of solid ice one hears and not the wail and crash and goblin sighing of moving ice floes such as one hears on the wintry St. Lawrence below the Isle of Orleans. The sounds made by the pond are sounds of power moving in bondage, of force constrained within a force and going where it can. The ice is taking up, settling, expanding, and cracking across though there is not a sign of all this either from the hill above or from the shore.

What I first heard was a kind of abrupt, disembodied groan. It came from the pond . . . and from nowhere. An interval of silence followed, perhaps a half note or a full note long. Then across, again from below, again disembodied, a long, booming, and hollow utterance, and then again a groan.

Again and again came the sounds; the night was still yet never still. Curiously enough, I had heard nothing while busy in the barn. Now, I heard. Neither faint nor heavy-loud, yet each one distinct and audible, the murmurs rose and ended and began again in the night. Sometimes there was a sort of hollow oboe sound, and sometimes a groan with a delicate

15

undertone of thunder.

As I stood listening to the ice below, I became aware that I was really listening to the whole pond. There are miles of ice to the north and a shore of coves and bays, and all this ice was eloquent under the moon. Now east, now west, now from some far inlet, now from the cove hidden in the pines, the pond cried out in its strange and hollow tongue.

The nearer sounds were, of course, the louder, but even those in the distance were strangely clear. And save for this sound of ice, there seemed no other sound in all the world.

Just as I turned to go in, there came from below one curious and sinister crack which ran off into a sound like the whine of a giant whip of steel lashed through the moonlit air.

My old friends and neighbors, Howard and Agnes Rollins, used to tell me that the ice often spoke and groaned before a big storm. I must watch the glass and the wind and the northeast.

FARM DIARY

Somebody in a red suit of mackinaw cloth and a wool hat is on the pond, fishing through the ice for pickerel. In winter pickerel tend to lose their somewhat muddy taste. / Cold, dark and windless night, and the windows of farms across the pond throw paths of light upon the ice, paths blurred in outline and motionless, having none of the

16

life of the living water. / The last three nights having been rather arctic, I have been getting up at 3 A.M. to replenish the coal fire. The living room has been comfortably warm, and the outlying dependencies warmish, the core of heat fortifying the life of the sleeping house. / Elizabeth returns from a neighbor's with a present, a jar of mincemeat made from deer meat, a colonial recipe treasured on the farms.

The farm country is now a winter splendor of heavy woolens, a good, healthy-spirited display of mackinaws in bright colors, cheerful plaid shirts, and heavy woolen caps of plaided red, green, or royal blue. The pageant is at its best when snow has fallen, and the bright colors move about against a universal white.

Some scholar has said, and very wisely, that the songs of a people are an excellent token of their character. The student of human nature would do well to add their clothes! Let him meditate on the fact that in peasant countries where the earth is the real wealth, and the farm lives by its own farm prides and farm traditions, the costumes worn are the most vital, beautiful, and gay that have ever been seen in western civilization.

Conversely, the clothes of an industrial world are the most dreary, ugly, muddy clothes that a way of living has ever put on human backs. Look at them as they are worn by any average urban crowd. There is no sense of hope in them, nothing of life in any mood of pride. Sartorially, this is a new thing in human history. From the noble savage onward, man has been something of a gay dog.

I am glad that the north country goes in for clothes with life and color. It is an excellent sign. Which reminds me that if the neighbors see me wearing a particularly gorgeous new pair of hand-knitted yellow socks, they can recognize a Christmas present arranged for by Elizabeth.

III

There had been no sign of coming snow when I put the house to bed, turning down the oil lamps one by one and blowing them out as the flames sank low. Looking forth a moment from the kitchen door, all that I could discover was an overclouded darkness — no wind, no sound, no star. Sometime in the night, however, a howl of wind or sudden and glassy rattle of sleet must have reached me in my dreams for I got up quietly to see how things stood now that a northeast storm had risen in the night.

All winter long a lantern burns at night on the living room table, its wick turned only moderately low. It is a modern lantern, big, strong, and well-made, and I am grateful to it for the quiet and reassuring light it keeps for us through the dark.

The house was full of the sound of the gale. It was a winter northeaster, furious with wind and snow, and driving down against us from the dark and desolate North Atlantic and a thousand miles of whitecaps and slavering foam. Wailings and whistling cries, ghostly sighings under latched doors, fierce pushings and buffetings of the exposed walls — thrusts one could feel as a vibration of the house itself — all these had something of their being in the sheltered and humanly-beautiful room. United with these, tumultuous and incessant, rose the higher aerial cry of the gale in space above the earth.

Our little dog lay in his basket close by the coal fire. Opening his eyes, he looked at me with both recognition and inquiry, and then with a sigh composed himself again to sleep. I found the kitchen growing cold, for the wood fire in the range had died away to a bed of ash and a few sparks. Having plenty of kindling, I soon had a new fire going, and it caught at once for the great chimney was still warm.

A pair of windows over the sink face the east and the pond, and these were under the full attack of the storm. Volleys of sleet were striking against them, wild gust by wild gust, and great flakes were sliding down the panes. Every now and then I could hear, even through the wind, the sound which snow makes against glass — that curious, fleecy pat and delicate whisper of touch which language cannot convey or scarce suggest.

Timber and wall, the old, honest, well-built house resisted with its own defiance. It has closed with such storms for almost one hundred and fifty years, standing in its ancient fields as a fortress of the hopes of man and his will to live. An old farm is always more than the people under its roof. It is the past as well as the present, and vanished generations have built themselves into it as well as left their footsteps in the worn woodwork of the stair.

The lantern, now turned higher, shone peacefully from the kitchen table and the red-check tablecloth. The room was getting very comfortably warm though a blast as from the pole was blowing in under the door leading north into the shed. Picking up an old hooked rug, I blocked the gust as best I could.

It was five o'clock, and still night, and the tumult unabating. By noon we should be snowed in. Treks to the spring would have to be made on snowshoes for as one flounders about and struggles ahead in deep snow, it is easy to lose one's footing and sit down in a drift — pail, water, and all. Where, I thought, are the wild creatures in this wilderness of night and flying snow? The deer would be "yarded up" somewhere in the lonelier regions of the big woods, each group making its own "yard" and keeping the snow down by moving round. The great, ungainly moose would shelter somehow in their hiding places. I remembered what strange sheltered vales and hide-aways one can come upon in the forest, and how still they can seem even when the wind is high.

A vagueness of light began to appear. Streaming south across the west field, the snow passed in vast billows and strange, wavering curtains whose heights were concealed in the mystery overhead. It would be a wild day.

A pleasant and rosy morning full of the vast silence of the winter countryside and marked by the lowest temperature we have yet had. / Home again from a visit to friends in town, home again, and glad to be back where everything doesn't come into the house along a wire or down a pipe. What a relief it was to get into my farm clothes and have a reasonable amount of physical work to do! / A friend on the salt water reports that a flight of snowy owls has just passed along the coast. / Snowing hard, and as I carry my pail of spring water across the field, the huge flakes drop in, spreading out grey just within the surface and then vanishing. / My friend Bob Smith tells me that in the old lumbering days there were bells on all the teams to give warning of their coming along the narrow, winding roads. Elizabeth found one of these very bells last summer and gave it to our neighbor Irving for his two big white horses, Major and Prince. They were wearing it today on their double harness, and very pleasant it was to hear the sweet and mellow jingle coming from the woods.

When the nineteenth century and the industrial era took over our western civilization, why was it that none saw that we should all presently become peoples without a past? Yet this is precisely what has happened and it is only now that the results of the break have become clear.

The past is gone, together with its formal arts, its rhetoric, and its institutions, and in its place there has risen something rootless, abstract, and alien, I think, to human experience. Nothing of this sort has ever occurred in history.

I do not feel so bewildered when I return to my own fields. The country cannot avoid being a part of its own era, the abstract world is about us, yet we are not without a past and never shall be. For us the furrow is the furrow since the beginning of the world, and the plough handles are to our hands what they were to those who cleared the land. Linked with this past, moreover, is all the human past of man as a part of Nature, of one living by the sun and the moon, and waiting for the clearing in the west.

IV

It is the full midwinter, the season of snow, ear-tingling cold, and skies into whose blue the earth reflects back its own intensity of light. It is not heat but light which is returning to the world, and so glittering is the morning air and so cloudless the sky that the sun rolls up over the eastern woods like a sudden miracle of radiant gold, borrowing no red from the lower atmosphere.

No sound is more characteristic of this leafless time than the cries of blue jays from the nearer woods and the trees and buildings of the farm. Again and again, when I am busy out of doors, I hear that single screaming call across the wilderness of snow. I hear it just as the austere shadows of winter are coming to life with the sunrise, I hear it, and hear it answered, through the bright hollow of high noon. There is as yet no touch of spring in the note; it is the familiar harsh call and nothing more. Yet to us on the farms it is music for it means that life in the air, daring, vigorous, and even jocular, is sharing the winter with us, and has not fled from us before the deep bitterness of cold.

I do not see many blue jays as I work in sum-

24

mer in the fields. Avoiding the vicinity of the house and our nearer trees, they set up housekeeping in such hardwood areas as have grown up between old pasture land and the pines. Every old farm in the region has such groves of maple, oak, and beech. From such a vantage, they forage the outer fields and their own preferred woodland, seldom, if ever, going down into the deep evergreen forest. It is the more simple-minded flicker who goes into the hemlocks and pines, and only too often do I find in forest openings the woeful heap of brownish and yellow feathers which mark a tragedy for one creature and a dinner for the other.

With the lengthening of autumn, the jays forsake their summer haunts and move down closer to the farms. It is then that one sees them in some near-by apple tree, hopping about with that fine, vigorous jump they know how to manage. Towards the end of the year, the birds again wander away. I rarely see or hear them during January. But with February and the return of the light comes the flash of blue, and a first salute to the earth and the sun reborn.

Yesterday afternoon, while calling on a neighbor, I saw by his barn a sight I look for every year. He had been shaking hay down from his lofts, and had then taken his broom, and swept the chaff and hay-dust out upon the snow. The day was the very quintessence of the winter, a time of pure, universal blue and pure, universal white. In the full sunlight and the snow, my neighbor's neighbors had come to share the bounty of the team. Five vigorous and gaudy jays were flying back and forth between a bit of fence rail adjoining the barn and the chaff-covered snow, a wonderful sight to see from scarcely ten feet away.

On the snow itself, prospecting and frisking in the chaff, their heads lowered, their bushy tails twitching, were two grey squirrels. Sometimes the jays and squirrels, grey fur and blue feathers all in company, were gathered together on the ground. Only once did I see the jays fly in a group to the fence top, and that was when the old farm cat passed them on her way into the barn. I could not see that she paid the slightest attention to the guests.

Ornithologists are given to scolding the jay, and accusing him of piratical behavior. We do not have the magpie in the east, but the jay is a close relative, and it is apt to be a rather mischievous family. But who could really be angry, and at such a time, with so handsome, "rugged," and American a bird? In a few weeks I should be hearing the spring note, that really musical and plaintive call which will mark the turning of the first corner of the year.

FARM DIARY

Yesterday in the cold and solitary winter twilight, I came upon a yoke of Holstein steers hauling an unloaded lumber sledge through the deep snow. Their driver, a middle-aged man, walked beside them in the dusk, all three pushing their way ahead along the unbroken road. / Every year the frost "heaves" the kitchen ell up about an inch and a half, the actual ell sliding up the fixed chimney like a ring on a finger. One latch no longer closes properly, and I shall have to readjust it. / From a sky full of sunshine but veiled to the west with a mere gauze of cloud descends the smallest snow I have ever seen, snow tiny as the dust of mica people buy to scatter on Christmas trees. It is falling with a brilliant and rather artificial twinkle through the sunlit air. / Elizabeth says that during the recent snowstorm, some half a dozen redpolls were perched on the tall weed stalks to the lee of the barn.

The secret of snow is the beauty of the curve. In no other manifestation of Nature is the curve revealed in an almost abstract purity as a part of the visible mystery and splendor of the world. What I think of, as I set down these lines, is the intense and almost glowing line which a great dune of snow lifts against the blue radiance of the morning after a storm, that high, clear, and incomparable crest which is mathematics and magic, snow and the wind. How many times have I paused to stare at such a summit when I have found it barring my way at a turn of the unploughed country road! It is when winds are strong, temperatures low, and the snow almost powder dry that you will see such monuments of winter at their best. Dunes of sand obey the same complex of laws, but the heavier sand does not have the aerial grace of the bodiless and radiant crystal which builds the snow against the sky.

V

The snow of the great storm still lies upon the landscape, the striations and erosions of its flattened surface still testifying to both the strength and the direction of the gale. Higher and higher across the south, the brilliant sun of March climbs to a noonday which is now clear of the higher branches of our dooryard trees, and from the kitchen chimney of the farm a faint pillar of blue, almost imperceptible smoke dissolves into the air. The wind is due west, cold as it blows across the snow, and the temperature is a little above freezing. Looking towards the sunlight and over the crust of purest white, I notice the chimney smoke at the next farm suddenly thicken and grow heavier: someone in the kitchen has just put a fresh stick on the fire.

It is a day to be busy out of doors and to come in only to warm one's hands. A real sense of life is in the shining air, the earth stirs in its winter sleep, and the great solar energy by which we live is striking down with power into this iron-hard crust of earth and snow.

What has today taken my interest are the colors in our winter world. There is color seen and unseen everywhere about: the universe is no duality of white and blue, and were I to stop and stare about awhile, I know that I should see more than I now see in a casual glimpse. In the landscape near at hand both grey trees and brown together with white birches rise above the snow; between me and the sun are faraway stone walls whose shadows are almost black; to the west, the pines stand dark, and withered and rusty autumn is still discoverable along the borders of the fields. At a turn of the farm road, moreover, I know there stands a copse of brush which during the deep of winter has turned itself into a thicket of red twigs whose color becomes a strange coral after a night of ice and freezing rain.

Surely the most beautiful of all colors of winter is the blue of winter shadows on the snow! It is a blue which varies with the day and the light, but whatever its tone, is both tender and delicate, and to see it is to be reminded of the purity of certain blues in flowers.

About an hour ago, I had a small adventure in this mystery of blue. A stone's throw from our gate, the farm road climbs a rather steep twenty-foot rise, and one coming from the south sees the gate and the top of the knoll against the northern sky. I had been down to visit my neighbors, Carroll and Louise, and as I walked home up the knoll I saw by the gate the shadows of our white birches on the snow, an open pool of snow water in the road, and the northern sky above and beyond. For a moment, as I plodded ahead, this was all I really saw.

Then, even as I looked, something touched me on the shoulder with a new awareness, and the scene became transformed. The shadows which were but shadows turned to pools of a deep gentian blue, a color tranquil and serene, and the water, which had been but water in a snow pool close beside the shadows, became a mirror of some blue and glowing vault of heaven — this other blue being as pure as the first, but perhaps more bright, and with the brightness a measure more delicate. By contrast the sky beyond both the pool and the winter shadows appeared more green. The sun shone, there was no sound, and there was I standing in the road and staring at two of the most beautiful appearances of color in Nature which I think I have ever seen. Only a ridge of purest white snow separated the shadows from the pool.

It was as if Nature, in the depth of our austere winter, had called into being the delicate colors of a garden. I shall long remember this small adventure by the gate.

FARM DIARY

The northeast gale which recently swept the coast, arriving with the dark of Sunday evening and blowing great guns all the long hours of the night, did more damage than we had at first suspected. Trees were wrenched and broken, windows blown in,

31

and I hear of barns having been partially unroofed. Our own small neighborhood did not fare badly, and I am glad to be able to set down that the entire crew was rescued from the freighter ashore on Cape Elizabeth. / The sun and the clock of life will presently be stirring the hibernating animals in their secret hideaways contrived within this earth, each small, faint heartbeat beginning to quicken in response to the new unseen splendor overhead. / Starlight on the fields of snow and all the windless sky a miracle of stars, and as Elizabeth and I walk out to see the rising of Arcturus, we hear a first owl hooting from the woods: "object, matrimony." / Wood and coal holding out unusually well but I am glad that the living year is coming our way. / A quiet, warmish, cloudy morning with a smell of woodsmoke in the air from a neighbor's brushpile burning furiously above the snow.

One aspect of the machine world which has not had sufficient attention is the relation of the machine age to the mystery of human joy. If there is one thing clear about the centuries dominated by the factory and the wheel, it is that although the machine can make everything from a spoon to a landing-craft, a natural joy in earthly living is something it never has and never will be able to manufacture. It has given us conveniences (often most uncomfortable) and comforts (often most inconvenient) but human happiness was never on its tray of wares. The historical result of the era has been an economic world so glutted with machine power that it is being shaken apart like a jerry-built factory, and a frustrate human world full of neurotic and ugly substitutes for joy.

Part of the confused violence of our time represents, I think, the unconscious search of man for his own natural happiness. He cannot live by bread alone and particularly not by sawdust bread. To speak in paradox, a sense of some joy in living is one of the most serious things in all the world.

VI

A strong and almost sandy crust has surfaced over the wintry countryside of snow. For three and even four steps, it bears one's weight like a white floor, and then, alas, it cracks, and one plunges through almost to the knee. As it is too glassy to be comfortable under snowshoes, and one cannot walk with much ease, we keep to our ploughed roads and shoveled paths and make the best of it. Held in its bright tension by the cold, and little troubled by the wind, the vast and shining floor is not without its own interest. For one thing, it is on such a surface that one can observe the shadows of winter which are unlike all other shadows of the year.

Summer is the season of motion, winter is the season of form. In summer everything moves save the fixed and inert. Down the hill flows the west wind, making wavelets in the shorter grass and great billows in the standing hay; the tree in full leaf sways its heavy boughs below and tosses its leaves above; the weed by the gate bends and turns when the wind blows down the road. It is the shadow of moving things that we usually see, and the shadows are themselves in motion. The shadow of a branch, speckled through with light, wavers across the lawn, the sprawling shadow of the weed moves and sways across the dust.

The shadows of winter are astronomical. What moves them is the diurnal motion of the sun. The leafless tree may shudder through its boughs, and its higher twigs and small branches sway a little to and fro, but of that gaunt and rigid motion only a ghost of movement trembles on the snow beneath. Tree-trunk and tree shape, the bird house and its pole, the chimney with its ceaseless smoke, the dead and nodding golden-rod — the life of their shadows comes with sun-rise and with sunset dies. All day long beneath these winter suns, each austere and simplified image slides glancingly from west to east with the slow and ordained progress of the dial shadow on the wall.

Today having been spent outdoors from early morning to the close of afternoon, it is these shadows I have been watching on the hardened snow. They seem to me one of the most charac-teristic features of the winter, and I wonder that so little is said about them by dwellers in the country.

Today's tree shadows began with the image long, aslant, and blurred. The clearer and more definite shadow-image is always near the trunk, close, that is, to the object by which the shadow is cast. At noon, I thought, there came the maxi-mum of definition. The sun is still rather low, and the shadow reached out from the tree much more than it would in June. As the afternoon lengthened, the shadows of the higher branches, always a little blurred, grew more indistinct, leaning to the east. The whole image died away on the snow in the winter twilight smouldering in the cloud-haze to the west.

I have not the painter's eye, but I could see that the shadows were blue even as the painters show them and that the blue varied in intensity. That night, I went out awhile to watch the moon shadows which again are astronomical, and thought certain aspects of the tree images perhaps more definite than those I had seen by day.

The moon is now very high. Utterly silent, the huge landscape, glazed with the moon, rolled on under the heavens, the shadows foreshortened and falling due north. It might have been the phantom of a summer day.

FARM DIARY

Monday before sunrise, and the windows glazed with ferns and opaque mysteries of ice, all turning a glowing crystalline rose as the hidden sun clears the tree tops to the east. / Across the west field from somewhere in the forest comes the sound of the axe, the blows falling rhythmic, heavy, and dully wooden across the frozen air. / On a glorious day after a light snow, "Mrs. B." and I have a winter picnic on the shore of the pond, our cooking fire burning on the top of a great rock just emerging from last week's drifts, the flame blown furiously by capfuls of the northwest wind; temperature six above. / On a grey and steely day, with snow clouds lowering, a great, steel-colored truck comes rolling along over the pond to where three men are busy cutting ice — the worked area marked off by little bushy firs. / Have received from Denver, Colo., a fine warm pair of western-style long pants made from government kersey. As they narrow below the knee, they fit particularly well with our high boots and heavy stockings. / Smelts running fairly well in the salt rivers, and baskets of freshly caught dozens for sale in various stores.

The seed catalogues are arriving again, and as I take them from their brown envelopes and study them at the kitchen table, I muse again on the dogmatic assertion which I often make that the countryman's relation to Nature must never be anything else but an alliance. Alas, I know well enough that Nature has her hostile moods, and I am equally aware that we must often face and fight as we can her waywardness, her divine profusion, and her divine irrationality. Even then, I will have it, the alliance holds. When we begin to consider Nature as something to be robbed greedily like an unguarded treasure, or used as an enemy, we put ourselves in thought outside of Nature of which we are inescapably a part. Be it storm and flood, hail and fire, or the yielding furrow and the fruitful plain, an alliance it is, and that alliance is a cornerstone of our true humanity.

VII

Among the various things which vanish into the vast emptiness of winter, the countryman counts the presence of water as a living and flowing power of the earth. The waters of earth which began flowing in the cold northern spring, making each greater gully of the woods the bed of a small brook and turning regions of the fields to sodden mires — where are they now in this temperature? Where is their sound in this great silence of the cold?

There are no rills flowing anywhere about, and what puddles may have come into being from some midday warmth are mere hollows and kettle-holes of solid ice. Water thrown out at the barn freezes before the eyes. The earth and the fountains of earth are sealed in iron.

All, I shall have to say, save one living voice — that of the overflowing well-spring of the farm. Those of the past who found it came upon no visible rill but only upon a small depression in which water-loving grasses grew comfortably in the hottest summers, surrounded by brown and thirsty hay.

Digging down some ten feet, they came upon a granite ledge, over whose muddy top flowed from within a small but living stream. Some sixteen years ago, I had the reservoir enlarged and walled about to make a roofed pit some ten feet square, the overflow outlet opening towards the pond.

I know no other such living rill in the nearer countryside. Huge storms bury the outlet under their deeps and masses of snow, new snows and the alternate warmth and cold of day and night cover it with a pebbled roof of ice a foot thick, low temperatures beard the oak pipe with gigantic icicles, and still the water flows. I have never known the winter rill to fail.

Every morning I go to it for a fresh pail of drinking water. The spring is only a comfortable minute's walk north into the fields. I use a white enamel pail, and save time by lifting off the hatchway of the spring-house and taking the water directly from the pit.

So radiant pure it comes, so much like a welling of light, that there are times — as indeed this morning — when the filled pail, nested in the snow, might be empty as when I carried it from the door.

How cold it was on the slope! The great pond is a pond no more, but a level of deep snow traced by strange, wavering paths of the wind. Months will pass before I hear again the familiar murmur from the rocky shore. Only the small tinkle of the living spring, seemingly without companion in the earth, remains of all the sound of waters, the treble music mingling unchanged with the lonely crying of the wind.

FARM DIARY

After a great snow storm, three pairs of snowshoes stand in a drift outside a friend's kitchen door; the neighbors have dropped in for a call. / On a morning bright with a glassy wind and full of whirled-up dust of snow, the welcome snow plough comes in sight, everybody aboard the truck bundled up in heavy clothes like winter bears, the hardy, outdoor faces glowing with the cold. A youngster home from Iceland walks behind, a shovel over the shoulder of his Navy pea-jacket, and bright red "protectors" on his ears. / To town on a cold day, finding various cars frozen up and snorting steam like dragons, the smell of radiator alcohol strong along the sidewalk. One car radiator is covered over with quite a good patchwork quilt. / How pleasant it is to get home from such a trip, and find the house warm, sunlit, and at peace, the last of a great stick of wood still glowing in the kitchen stove! Standing beside the range, Elizabeth meditatively warms her hands.

The chromium millenium ahead of us, I gather, is going to be an age whose ideal is a fantastically unnatural human passivity. We are to spend our lives in cushioned easy chairs, growing indolent and heavy while intricate slave mechanisms do practically everything for us as we loll.

What a really appalling future! What normal human being would choose it, and what twist of the spirit has created this sluggish paradise? No, I do not mean that we should take the hardest way. Compromises are natural and right. But a human being protected from all normal and natural hardship simply is not alive.

VIII

Supper had been cleared away, the dishes done, and the peaceful, lamplit kitchen restored to its evening simplicity. Because the night was cold, we lingered by the cosier fire, Elizabeth deep in a book, and I going through those agricultural papers and magazines which had arrived for me since the beginning of the month. I am rather given to letting such mail accumulate, and saving the reading for a quiet night. Just as I was in the middle of an article, I remembered something I had forgotten in the barn. As there was nothing to do but go out and see to it, I shouldered into my blue reefer, picked up my lantern and turned to the door. And closing it behind me, I walked out into another world.

It was a night such as one sees perhaps half a dozen times a winter. The sky was less a sky of earth than interstellar space itself revealed in its pure and overarching height, an abyss timeless and remote and sown with an immense glittering of stars in their luminous rivers and pale mists, in their solitary and unneighbored splendors, in their ordered figures, and dark, half-empty fields. It was the middle of the evening and in the north over a lonely farm, a great darkness of the forest, and one distant light, the Dipper, stood on its handle, each star radiant in the blue and empty space about the pole.

These are the seven stars which come and go through the ages and the religions. Collectively known to the medieval past by the fine name of "The Plough," the configuration is today the Great Dipper to beholders, and gathered thus into a household and utilitarian shape, places something of our small humanity in the shoreless oceans of the sky.

The greater splendor burned white and blue above the south. There exalted and assembled in one immense principality of the skies, the shining press of the greater winter constellations glittered above the little cold and dark of earth. Orion, most beautiful of all the stellar figures, shone beyond the meridian, the timeless hunter of the timeless sky, Betelgeuse and Bellatrix burning on his shoulders and the triad of the belt about his waist. Sirius, lord of the ancient Nile and brightest of the stars, hung in his glorious and solitary place, the Bull with the reddened eye of Aldebaran charged some invader of his field of suns, and the matched stars of Gemini together with the planets Mars and Saturn formed themselves into a figure which astrologers might have watched and questioned through the night.

One stares awhile and then looks to earth for the reassurance which comes with the earthly and the near. What was left of a light snow lay starlit and pale, the vague and ragged regions of uncovered earth starlit too, yet half-lost in the dark. Fixed in such a starlit gloom, the barn raised its shadowy bulk to the light and the mystery overhead. In the more empty sky below Sirius, scattered stars shone through the branches of trees beside the road.

It was as I came from the team that I saw agriculture standing like a good omen above the fields. The starry plough had vanished from the imagination and the common language of man, but the remembered sickle stood high in the south and east and moved towards the meridian. Rolling on with all celestial space, the Lion of the zodiac followed great Orion, the fine if albeit left-handled sickle which the stars form glittering in the abyss, and at the base of the handle the great star Regulus, white, splendid, and serene.

Lower still, a new light trembled on the wooded ridge. It was Arcturus bringing with him that assurance of the spring and dedication of time for which the ancients used to wait in their warmer lands, Arcturus the great, the yellow star, loved of so many generations of men who live by bread.

FARM DIARY

Another snowfall and a fairly heavy one but the snow is going fast. / It is my impression that weekday radio programs are much less listened to here than they used to be. The

45

farms tune in for the weather reports and the news and then switch off. / The neighbors wonder if an incident similar to one described in Bambi may not have taken place in our woods. Last autumn we frequently saw a doe and her twin fawns. This doe was shot at the end of the hunting season, the fawns escaping. Some think that like Bambi these younglings rejoined their father for a fine buck has been seen several times in the woods, and on various occasions his tracks have been accompanied by the tracks of smaller deer. No one has actually seen the buck and the fawns together. / When the ice melts from the gutters and the snow from the valleys of the roofs, we hear the water flowing into the winter cistern under a corner of the kitchen. On quiet nights of warmish weather, it sounds like a little tinkling fountain hidden away beneath the floor.

How wise were the ancients who never lost sight of the religious significance of the earth! They used the land to the full, draining, ploughing, and manuring every inch, but their use was not an attack on its nature, nor was the ancient motherhood of earth ever forgotten in the breaking and preparing of the soil.

They knew, as all honest people know in their bones, that in any true sense there is no such thing as ownership of the earth and that the shadow of any man is but for a time cast upon the grass of any field. What remains is the earth, the mother of life as the ancients personified the mystery, the ancient mother in her robes of green or harvest gold and the sickle in her hand.

When farming becomes purely utilitarian, something perishes. Sometimes it is the earth life which dies under this "stand and deliver" policy; sometimes it is the human beings who practice this economy, and oftenest of all it is a destruction of both land and man. If we are to live and have something to live for, let us remember, all of us, that we are the servants as well as the masters of our fields.

IX

If the solar turn in December marks the return of light and the first great step forward of our northern year, something happens in February which the country man can only call the second great milestone of the annual rebirth. It is not a turn as definite as the solar reversal, but it is every bit as real and powerful. With us, it comes about February tenth, and even as I write, the mystery is upon us at the farm. It is the ritual moment when winter, still visibly unconquered, and even with weeks to go, has nevertheless lost the ascendancy, and the great vital forces appear and show themselves in a first promise of their power.

It is not entirely a matter of light, great as I believe the influence of light to be. It is not yet the rebirth of warmth for the sun as warmth does not come into power 'till the end of February. It is really a kind of entrance into action of the life forces, solar and terrestrial, a stirring, a shaking, and an awakening of all that will remake our cold and dormant world; as the Witch of Endor said to King Saul, "I see gods ascending out of the Earth."

I write this on a day in early March fierce with a northwest wind, and looking from the window out towards a night's new-fallen snow, I ask myself what signs have I of this turn which has no name? In the sunny window stands a box of experimental seedlings; before the soundings of the mysterious signal, before this metaphorical and cosmic crash of brass and cymbals in the empty air, they make but a little, creeping progress. Now they have taken a sort of green leap forward. Yesterday, talking over the change with my friend and neighbor Lester Dunbar, he said, "Everything responds to it. Now, I've noticed my brook year after year. Once the turn has come, the water begins to rise and run strong, even when there has been no thaw or sign of a thaw."

In chicken houses the eggs increase; even in the deeps of the sea, there is already a movement north along the coast. The green world would seem to follow the animal in point of time. In that kingdom and in this latitude, little or nothing of change is visible above the snow.

Perhaps the realm most aware of this — shall I say "Dionysian" turn? — is the wild life in our woods. Night and day now I hear foxes barking; the woods are full of them this year. Some think they have locally reduced the year's abundance of the "snowshoe rabbit," but I find about as many rabbit tracks as usual.

Only yesterday, a neighbor cutting wood in the forest heard a fox coming through the woods, the patter of his feet very audible on the crust. Every now and then, the creature barked. My neighbor hid behind a pair of hemlock trees. Just as he expected, the fox was on the old wood road, and coming in his direction. He came within about three feet of the trees, stopped, backed away, looked again, went a little farther off and looked for a third time. My neighbor now moved, and "My! You should have seen him go." A little later, the creature began barking again as he ran on. This story, too, I had from Neighbor Dunbar.

It is the time of the year when the foxes seek their mates. The wood stirs; there is hardly a night that we do not overhear some odd living sound or uneasy cry. The clock of the stars has struck, and life has awakened in the cold and has turned and has heard.

FARM DIARY

One of those giant rings whose diameter is approximately the length of the handle of the Dipper encloses the veiled moon together with the planets Mars and Saturn and the shoulders of Orion. Like a vast symbol or portent, it does not vanish with the hours but only changes position with the motion of the sky. / Elizabeth says that there are tracks on the overgrown road which must be those of the bobcat we have been hearing about. / General agreement among the farmers that automobile and tractor repairs are beginning to cost a lot of money — "if you can get the parts." / Early morning, and a bright, windless ten below. Find the cord at the spring, with which I lower my pail, frozen to a sort of thick, clumsy wire. Rather a job tying the usual knot!

One of the pleasantest things about country life is that it has never lost sight of the dignity of old age. To return to the farms from the city is to come from a region in which the really elderly have somehow vanished away to a region where human life and its natural human pattern are taken for granted. Here the work of the old is needed, and their opinions and ideas are listened to and valued. The old people do not feel themselves fifth wheels, nor are they left to themselves in some lonely rocking chair with nothing whatever to do, and no one really interested in what they have to say.

Again and again when business or a friendly call brings me to a farm, it is some "old-timer" who is turned to as the family weather prophet and as the authority on what ails the pig. It is "gramma" who sees both mother and the children through when they are ill, and once a fortnight bakes the "muster gingerbread" she has made for over sixty years. Very often, too, the old folks carry on busily and skillfully our country handicrafts. Among a number of such crafts, they make cane chairs, braid and hook wonderful rugs, and whittle toys. On a neighboring

51

island a fine old man close to ninety makes and repairs all the fishing nets and lobstering gear for his community.

No way of life is normal or even properly human without something of this kind. A denial of the conditions of existence cuts life in two. It is the rounding out which holds the adventure together, which gives it assurance, and establishes a communal wisdom and a memory.

X

Higher, higher climbs the radiant noonday sun, the shadows grow shorter beneath the trees, snow slides from the roof, and the shingles steam. March is a beautiful month in the north for now the battle is won, and we of the country world can take new storms and returning snows with an easier heart; they will soon be gone.

The very expression on our country faces has changed; we are released and expectant. Icicles meet and run, and gather to a fall of rainbow drops which make an incessant and crystal sound of tiny waters. A kind of seasonal pang shakes the whole earth.

All morning long, as I have worked in the sun with comfortable bare hands, a huge March wind has been rushing over the earth. It is a westerly wind rather than a northwester, but it might have come from any quarter of the compass. It has no name, this torrent of the air, it is but the wind. These March winds, I am told, mark something different in the calendar of the year, for they arise between an equator at its greatest heat and a polar region at its fiercest cold. They seem to me a little higher above the earth than the winds of early winter, for sometimes little stirs below on the winterish and thinly-muddy ground whilst the tops of the trees turn aside and cry out with a new cry in the great and day-long roaring.

The drifts have gone. The dead, brown wires of old spears of grass first pierced the vanishing snow, then widening tussocks rose, and last of all bare hilltops and southern slopes emerging. As the snow vanishes, the simplicity of the landscape disappears, and the eye wanders over a land spread out in springtime variegations of uncovered brown and ever-retreating white.

Walking this morning above the hay field, I noticed how residual snow still recorded last summer and its works, for the wheeltracks of the haycart were still traced in vestiges of snow, and there were lines of white in the ploughed land on the slope. Only the frozen pond gives no apparent sign of change and further change to come. It might be frozen forever into its frozen bays.

A few crows have returned: they visit us when the open earth appears. As my old friend and neighbor Mrs. Agnes Rollins said with a twinkle in her eye, "To think we'd ever be glad to see a crow!" A robin has been seen nearer the saltwater country, but so far there has been no sign of the wild geese.

All over the countryside there is a rush to finish winter chores. Cordwood must be got out on some last snow, and if needs be, some final layer of ice cut to fill the ice house to the top.

Of the four ancient and poetic symbols which haunted the imagination of the Scriptural East, the Eagle, the Lion, the Angel, and the Ox, the Eagle stood as the symbol of the East, the Morning, and the Spring. In this moment of blue sky and roaring wind, the wisdom of the poetry is borne in upon me, for it is the Eagle who is summoning and awakening the Morning and the Spring, his wings outstretched to the sun reborn and his talons gripped to the rock with ice on its shadowed side.

FARM DIARY

My woodshed beginning to look somewhat depleted, Lawrence Simmons comes to help me rebuild the stacks with wood stored under cover. Bulldozing a snowdrift with his truck, he fills up with a fine load, and soon we are both busy in the shed, the sliding door open to the western light. / Sad news of a returning veteran as related by a neighbor, "Yes, he's home but he's changed. Awfully changed. Why, he talks like a New Yorker." / The young women are great hands here for giving each other surprise birthday parties. As older friends we have just fallen heir to two pieces of birthday cake put aside for us in a wrapping of oiled paper. Elizabeth says that it is pink cake this time made with the syrup of preserved wild strawberries and that it looks particularly good.

No age in history can afford to lay too much emphasis upon "security." The truth is that from our first breath to our last we inhabit insecurely a world which must of its transitory nature be insecure, and that moreover any security we do achieve is but a kind of an illusion. While admitting that a profound instinct towards such safety as we can achieve is part of our animal being, let us also confess that the challenge involved in mere existence is the source of many of the greater virtues of human character.

XI

Every once in a while, and in good snowshoeing weather, I go down into my woods to look at the tracks of the wild creatures and see what we have for neighbors. We live on a kind of mitten-shaped peninsula in a pond, and our woods begin at the stony, overgrown backbone of the area, and grow down a rather steep slope to the secluded cove which gives us a second shoreline to the west.

The woods are at once farm country and the old forest of the north. White pines and hem-locks predominate and make it an evergreen country, some of our bigger pines being miracu-lous survivors of the great primeval growth. I imagine that these would have been "mast pines" in the old ship building days, for they tower green above the other tree-tops, straight as the "sticks" of a full-rigged ship.

I have hardwood, too, rock maple, yellow birch, red oak, and beech, which we cut for our winter fires. In one secluded nook stands a su-perb primeval ash, beautiful as the tree of Odin, Yggdrasil, which held the worlds together.

The last time I visited the woods, the snow lay deep. All winter long, new snow had fallen on old, mingling the surfaces into one heavier depth and mass of white. Entering the region, I took the farm track whose beginning is a natural arch of pine boughs through which one sees a mild slope leading down into woods. The snow deepened, the light changed, and something more hushed took the place of the open light and the larger sound.

To each side, beyond the trunks of the bordering trees, the beautiful, delicately-shadowed snow lay with a surface but a few days old and still light because of the low temperatures. Far and near, the wind and snow had scattered it over with a dust of bark and tiniest fallen twigs, with broken-off tufts of needles from the white pines, and with a green and universal rain of the terminal twigs of hemlocks. At one place a familiar spring had welled up through the white and was flowing across the wood road and downhill in a vein of living water and uncovered earth.

As I "mushed" on into a little clearing, walking towards the sun, I had a glimpse of a winter effect I always like to see. On the tops of the trees the wind was blowing, and just ahead of me there suddenly fell from a hemlock branch a quantity of snow which disintegrated to powder in the sunlit air. As it thus dissolved, the snow dust turned to a mist of rainbow brilliance, a certain coppery, bronzy glow seeming to hang for a moment against the sun.

There were tracks everywhere, the most common being those of the "snowshoe rabbit" — really the varying hare, and the fox. This northern and arctic hare has its familiar name from the tracks its huge forefeet leave in the snow, and very like the prints of small snowshoes they are, even to an occasional comic suggestion of the pattern of the weave. His arch enemy the fox, too, had been everywhere about, that direct, purposeful single line now crossing the road, now following it awhile, now leading off into the more open growth.

Animals use our human roads almost as much as we do. I came upon hardwood trees with a woodsy litter beneath them, and marked where various grey squirrels had drawn upon their reserves of food; but saw squirrel tracks most often near the old stone-walls. A porcupine had followed a lesser wood-road a good half mile — taking all the shortcuts! — and a small deer had gone down the side of a hill, the divided hoof mark very clearly imprinted where the snow lay windswept and thin.

Of the makers of the tracks, I saw nothing. Calling to each other like school children, I heard chickadees in a kind of sunlit glen, and when I came out of the woods, one watched me from a young hemlock and sang his greeting.

FARM DIARY

"Did you catch anything?" I asked a friend who had returned from pickerel fishing through the ice. "Yes, four and a cold." /

59

The owls are beginning to hoot in the woods. The great horned owl winters here, and in the depth of winter hoots before a thaw; it is almost a sure sign. When spring draws near, the owls hoot, thaw or no thaw. / There is an old expression in use here for a snowstorm which comes after the spring robins return: we call it a "robin storm." I was amused the other night to hear the participle "suppering" — "You can get Bill while he's suppering over to his brother's." / Elizabeth has gone on a week-end visit to her sister's, leaving the house well-stocked and everything comfortable, but the little dog and I both think that the whistle of next Monday's arriving train will be a very pleasant sound.

A few days before the Vernal Equinox we have a kind of special celebration in the farm kitchen and at breakfast time. The kitchen, as I have said, is in the ell of the house, and because on one side the windows face due east, we have for the greater part of the year the awakening and refreshing presence of the morning sun. As October draws near, the great disk, moving south, with every sunrise draws nearer a corner of the main house extended beyond the ell and cutting off our view to the southeast.

Nearer and nearer to the fated corner moves the great lamp, nearer and nearer, turns it, and the kitchen does not have morning sunlight till long months have worn away.

If we were people of the Golden Age and the Golden Bough, we would get our pipes and timbrels, our long trumpets of bronze, and our other musical what-have-yous ready for March fifteenth. On that morning the sun, which has been steadily approaching the corner, turns it, the golden round rising clear of all obstruction and flooding the kitchen with the first spring light. It is for us an occasion of real joy. We may not belong to the Golden Age or the years of the Golden Bough, but we can observe and rejoice, and in such natural joy and natural response lies one of the profoundest secrets of human happiness.

XII

Cheered by the increasing light and a long spell of pleasant weather, "up March hill" we go, to use an old phrase which is still very much alive among us. The fields on every side remain in possession of our long winter, but in the shelter of the south wall of the house the short, dead grass of the farmhouse lawn is coloring through with the first tranquil green of the new year.

Beyond the pale fields, the evergreen forest is losing its winter austerity. Massed together on a pasture hill, the pines prepare the resinous, green-fleshed "candles" of new growth which will so suddenly burst forth just as our short-lived spring promises to turn to summer; the hemlocks, meanwhile, making ready their branchlet ends of yellow-green.

Winter may hold the chilly surface of our northern soil, but beneath the snow, and in the timeless dark below the frost, the forest is waking to the hunger of life, and the fine roots are asearch in the cold clays and the crumbles of granite and the mould.

The faith of the earth in itself never falters, and in the woods this is the secret and hidden season of the triumph of life. The fierce courtships of last autumn, the pursuits, the wooings, the escapes, reluctances, and yieldings, bear their fruit in this bleakness and light of early spring.

The red fox mothers her eager, sharp-nosed cubs whilst the male ranges our woodpaths to feed his mate and the milk hunger of the brood; the doe turns to her fawn and nuzzles it to its feet; the she-bear's cubs, tiny as kittens when born in the earlier winter, shake off the strange half-life, half-sleep which they have shared with their mother and now begin to utter louder cries and tumble about in their caves in the vast woodlands of the north.

I think of all this when the sun goes down beyond the roof of my barn, and the woods darken against the bleak gold of the March sky. Behind that almost conspirational wall of young pines and the older pines above, what faith in life works with intensity towards life and the continuance of life. What tenderness there must be in that world without speech, what power of courage, sacrifice, and endurance. So goes on the life of the forest, and meanwhile great Orion slopes his shoulders to the west.

FARM DIARY

Smelting season on the salt rivers drawing to a close, what there is of ice growing day by day more unsure, and large floes breaking off with every tide. / Blue jays very noisy in

63

their frontier world midway between the hayfields and the deep woods, and I often hear the sweet, bell-like note one associates with spring. / As the earth clears of snow, skunks emerge, and on warmish mornings after warmish nights, I often come upon the small, delicate tracks in the thin mud enclosing roadbed puddles. / Good farm-country Sunday dinner at a friend's, chicken stew with dumplings, various fixings such as cole-slaw and "sour dressing," a mashed turnip dish baked in the oven with cheese and a noble choice between a pie of deer-meat mince and a pumpkin pie with a wavy crust. / Spring food-sales now being held in the various church basements, and Elizabeth provides us with a box of "brownies" of the blond, brown sugar kind which turn out to be rapturously good. / Wood and coal holding out unusually well, but I am glad that the living year is coming our way.

There is only one test of any political scheme or adventure in government. It is the quality of the human being produced by the political order and by the way of life occasioned by that order. Such materialistic arithmetic as the amount of electric power sold, the number of motor cars produced, and the immense potential of this and that means nothing whatever. A truce to these materialistic puffings of a materialistic heaven as vulgar, tedious, and empty in its conception as anything ever held up to the inquiring spirit of man.

But the human being? There you are. Is that human being a conscious member of a community and willing to do his best by it, has he honesty and courage, the reasonable public good manners which keep the experiment on the way it should go, has he a proper sense of the human decencies and is he seized upon now and then by his birthright of natural gaiety; has the man his quality of manhood and decision and the woman her immense and mystical power?

"Man the measure of all things." A good adage once the limits of its application are understood. Let's have it again on a few doorways and temple pediments.

XIII

It has always been our custom to take a little stroll before we put the house to bed, merely going to the gate and back when the nights are hostile with a bitterness of cold. Now that nights more mercifully human have come with the slow and dilatory spring, we go beyond the gate for perhaps a quarter or even half a mile, walking with miry feet down the farm road and through a sound of many waters.

Tonight under a faintly hazy sky and through a light wind one can feel but not hear, the winter is flowing downhill towards the still frozen and imprisoned pond. Out of the forests and the uplands a skein of rills is pouring, the small streams now seeking their ancient courses, now following an hour's new runner along the darkness of a wall.

So heavy is the hayfield soil, and so matted down with living roots below and thick dead grass above, that little earth seems to be lost anywhere, and for the moment there is no runner trying to make its way across ploughed land. But I have had my troubles in the past.

If the opening music of the northern year begins with a first trumpet call of the return of light, and the return of warmth is the second great flourish from the air, the unsealing of the waters of earth is certainly the third. As we walked tonight in a darkness from which a young moon had only just withdrawn, the earth everywhere, like something talking to itself, murmured and even sang with its living waters and its living streams.

Between us and the gate, a torrent as from an overflowing spring, half-blocked by a culvert heaved by frost, chided about our feet, and making another and smaller sound found its way downhill again in the night. Farther on, where woods close in to one side and the ground is stony and uneven, there tinkled out of the tree shapes and the gloom a sound of tiny cascades falling with incessant flow into a pool together with the loud and musical plashing of some newborn and unfamiliar brook.

Cold and wet, the smell in the spring air was not yet the smell of earth and spring. No fragrance of the soil, no mystery of vernal warmth hung above the farmland, but only a chill of sodden earth, water, and old snow. I knew that if I cared to look, I could find to the north of weathered ledges in the woods such sunken, grey-dirty, and gritty banks of ice as only the spring rains find and harry from the earth.

Yet spring somehow was a part of the night, the miry coldness, and the sound of water, a part of this reluctance of winter to break camp, a part of these skies with Sirius and Orion ready to vanish in the west. The long siege was broken, the great snows were over and gone, the ice was coming down from above tidewater in the current of the great rivers, and the colored twigs of the trees were at last awake.

Walking homewards towards the farm, now listening to the sound of water, now forgetting it as we talked, we both could see that much of the pond was surfaced with open water above its floor of ice. At the foot of our own hayfields a cove facing south and east showed in liquid and motionless dark, whilst beyond, and again above the ice, lay puddles and seas whose reflected quiet of starshine was a promise of the open water soon to come.

Across the pools, at the great farm on the hill, a light suddenly went out. Our own windows shone nearby, but we did not enter, so haunted were we both by the sense of the change in the year and the continuous sound of waters moving in the earth.

When we at length entered the house, using the side door and its tramped over and muddy step, we found ourselves welcomed by something we are very seldom aware of summer or winter — the country smell of the old house.

All old farms, I imagine, have some such rustic flavor in their walls; country dwellers will recognize what I mean. A hundred and fifty years of barrelled apples, of vegetables stored in a field-stone cellar, of potatoes in the last of the spring, of earth somewhere and never very far, of old and enduring wood and wood-smoke, too, and perhaps the faintest touch of mould from things stored long, long ago in a bin — all these and heaven knows what other farmhouse ghosts were unmistakably present in the neat room with its lamp and books. The cold and humid night had stirred the house as well as ourselves: it had its own rustic memories.

Elizabeth presently brought in two slices of apple pie and two glasses of cold milk, and for a first time I did not bother to build up the fire.

FARM DIARY

My friend Charles Bassett of Buffalo, N.Y., who is a leading authority on Indian corn and is now experimenting with a magnificent "rainbow" strain, tells me that when this particolored corn "is fed to chickens they always pick up the white and yellow kernels first, but when mice get an ear they eat the red kernels first." / With the warmer weather, the various sleepyheads and genuine hibernators are waking up, and yesterday, in a patch of mud between two patches of snow, I saw the unmistakable track of a woodchuck. Going about looking for a mate, I guess. / Some new species of owl has come to live in the neighborhood;

nobody has seen it, but we have all heard the unfamiliar hooting. / The pond has not yet opened, but all along the shore, between the ice floor and the land, lies a quiet width of open water calmly reflecting the spring sky.

The city has its heat and cold, its hunger and its thirst, but it has lost a great measure of the human birthright of physical sensation. Life there is so protected from Nature, so insulated, so to speak, that it ends up by being only a ghost of the human adventure. I say this because it has always seemed to me that a normal range of physical sensation, a sense, for instance, of the fabric of earth underfoot and the sudden cold of a change of the wind, is not only a part of the discipline of life but also of its reward.

XIV

Sodden and cold, the liberated earth rises from the long sleep and imprisonment of winter, her fields a yellowish pallor of water-soaked and matted grass, her roads a noonday glisten of mire and ruts of heavy mud. March with its snows and light and warmer temperatures can be one of the loveliest months of the year, but alas for early April and the long fortnight immemorially known as "mudtime." It is then that the "bottom falls out of the roads," as the local phrase has it, that cars get stuck and people try to pry them out with old boards and stones, and that paths of mud form on the linoleums which no scraping of feet at a doorstep can ever hope to cure.

"Mudtime" it is, mudtime up to our necks, and we shall all be bogged down, slowed down, be mud-booted and mud-breeched till the earth has yielded up its deeper frosts and dried in the mildly warm winds and the increasingly pleasant sun. The milk truck, however, seems to be managing it somehow, and I see cars lurch through with unexpected slides into mud soup and deep ruts which seize upon the tires and wiggle the steering wheel. When we meet, our ironic and universal phrase is this: "Nice weather overhead."

71

It is spring, and it is also the north, and we keep our fingers crossed while the season makes up its mind. Back and forth, between winter and summer, it goes, turning to winter and a sort of warm December with a cloud shadow and a searching wind, and then smiling back less to spring than to a promise of spring. We all rather grimly remember last year's blizzard on May eleventh, the wet, heavy snow on the apple orchards in blossom, and the consequent loss of almost the entire apple crop. But the farm house door stands open awhile towards the air and sun and a few flies have appeared who look as if they needed kind words and vitamins.

After a hard winter, this northern land is a kind of deserted battlefield. Seemingly lifeless itself and still cold, it shows on every side the wreckage of the long struggle and the obstinate withdrawal, the dead leaves decaying to rot and nothingness in the lifeless grass and the scattered twigs and branchlets becoming a part of the hungry life of nature and the soil.

The great winds of spring are both a pæan of victory and something of a farewell. Winter is gone and good riddance; it is indeed time for something else, yet even as I set down these words I remember the walk at night down into the woods after the great storm, the moonlight and the shadows in the clearings, the silence beyond all silences, and the evergreens laden and garlanded with snow.

Mudtime. Not much one can do outside the usual spring schedule of small jobs, repairs, plans, measurements, cogitations, and tinkerings. I'd like to be able to get down the farm bell, give it a sanding over, and then a new coat of gilt, but will have to wait till Lawrence comes to bear a hand.

The ice on the pond will certainly go within the next week. The path of open water about the central mass has appreciably widened, and lies there placid and rather dark; the residual ice itself darkening as the deep water beneath begins to show through. Robins and crows seem to be about our only birds. Crows are returning every day in greater numbers, and this morning I saw five walking about on the wet sod of the west field beyond the road.

Elizabeth says that a seagull came over earlier in the day, flying low over the woods, and bore south over the pond to a cove hidden in the pines. Seagulls do not visit us in winter, and this is the first seafarer of the ploughman's year.

FARM DIARY

This is not a sugar-bush country, but we do have sugar maples, and here and there a farmer is trying to make a few quarts of syrup for family use. All kinds of make-do containers hang from the trees, such as lard pails, preserve jars, and even milk bottles rigged with a wire. This small scale syrup which is boiled down on the kitchen stove is usually pretty good, for it keeps something of the wild tang — not too confoundedly pure. / No more frost on the panes and I can now see the outdoor world when I get things going in the morning. When every window is opaque with frost, the house is a kind of sealed fortress, and oneself a kind of prisoner. / Spring call of the blue jays very frequent now; sounds like a note blown from an old-fashioned "organ whistle" made of seasoned wood. / My friend "Chad" Richards of Camden tells me that on a pond to the north he followed an otter track for miles on a surface of light snow, the track very distinct, and "one foot bled a little." The creature made a great circle like a fox and deliberately went through every "wet, slushy puddle" on the ice.

Whenever I visit a farm where there are little children below school age, I am always interested to see how naturally and easily the farm leads them on into its own pattern of farm and family life. On a farm, the day's work is the most exciting and interesting thing that goes on, and farm children are instinctively aware of it, deserting their toys on the instant to rush out and see Buttercup's new calf. The boys start imitating farm work early and may want to feed the stock before they can scarce walk, the little girls very quickly come to a knowledge of their own power and their own skills. Imperceptibly and sometimes very fast, the "help" ceases to be play, and the first thing you know you have a farmer.

I know well enough that it does not always work this way, and that the farm can produce a rebel and a hard case as well as any environment. But the principle is the right one, and the road an honest and human path. There is something very fine in family labor shared together in good-will by all the generations under a roof. It holds the household together in a bond of life and a unity of purpose, it gives a human core of strength, and it builds up a family against time and loneliness.

One morning last October when I was splitting wood by the barn, a boy of five whose uncle was working with us that day came over to me and very quietly and without a word began to sort out billets of the size I was splitting and lay them by my hand. He stood by and helped me as long as I worked there, neither of us breaking a polite reticence, but both of us entirely at ease, companionable, and content. His people were not rich in the world's goods, but he was already a little friendly human being prepared to do his share and glad to be doing it. I shall never forget the grave friendliness and quiet goodwill of that small child.

XV

Three days of warmish spring weather and three days of bottomless mud, and now comes a morning of cold and glaring light with the northwest wind blowing the chimney smoke of the wood fires. The pine branches on the pasture hill roll and sway, the tops of the trees restlessly nodding, and over the dead grass fly last year's oak leaves in their familiar panic before the invisible streaming of the air.

The wind is neither high nor keen, it is only blustery and comfortably cold. Out of the region of the sky called "the eye of the wind" it comes, and looking thither, I see there a blue clarity and even a cold luminousness as of a window into outer space.

Over the grass, over the roofs and the house, the eddies gather and sweep on, each great sigh trailing behind it a silence which is never a full hush. Only the pond remains in grim quiescence. Still frozen, it lies at the foot of our slopes like an obstinate nugget of winter, the ever-thinning surface changing color with the depth of ice, the vagaries of temperature, and the differing hues of the sky.

The winter's two-foot floor was no such mirror, and under any sky had an austere look which was all its own. But this ice! Yesterday morning, after a sharp night, the pond emerged from the darkness a new and glassy white, a milk-onyx white, and this it kept till early afternoon when it took on a greyness of mush snow. By evening it had gone steely, darkening to another strange color without any quality or vibration of life.

Obstinate relic of winter, when will it be gone? Not "till the pond is open" will this cold and muddy earth waken to its own life under the already awakened sky. There is a country saying here, and a sound one, that the frost is never fully out of the ground till the ice is out of the pond. When will it go this year? When will it turn that strange blue which is the signal of its disappearance? I have seen the pond open on the twenty-sixth of March — the earliest date anyone can remember — I have seen it stay frozen till April was almost at its end.

Had I not stopped yesterday to study the pond, to "stand and stare" as Davies says, I would have missed something I hope to have a sight of every spring.

Friends had told me that the geese were going north. My neighbor Elwell Oliver saw a flock go over March fifteenth, a little after midday. Another neighbor whose farm is on a hill heard them last week "hollering" overhead as he went to his team in the early dark. Because our lakes are frozen, the geese here follow the coast, and settle down for a spell in the open, salt water estuaries and tidal reaches of our great freshwater streams. I have seen them by the hundreds in the coves and sheltered by-waters of the Kennebec and the Penobscot, making themselves at home there well on towards the end of spring.

There is a kind of sixth sense which gives one a nudge now and then, and it was probably that sense which prompted me to look at the sky while I was studying the pond. The geese had come from behind, from the west southwest, and there they were, just overheard, in a sky without a single cloud, in a sky all light and springtime blue. It was a large flock, and the birds were flying rather high in a marked but irregular "V." I heard no "hollering," not a note of that lovely, bell-like chorusing which so stirs the heart when a great flock of Canada geese go over in the early night.

Over the pond they went and on towards a ridge lying almost due northeast. I could see them as they cleared it, melting away in the sky above the farms and trees as a faint and wavering line. I looked at my watch; it was a few minutes after four o'clock, and the shadows on the steely lake were themselves turning steely on the ice.

FARM DIARY

Morning sunlight, a cold north wind, vast, vague clouds, snow-flurries, and sunlight again, the whole drama began and ended in

78

twenty minutes. / During the war years some of the hay could not be cut for lack of labor, and people burned over the acreage in the spring. Last night, under a splendor of the Northern Lights, a soldier-farmer who has taken a place on a hilltop burnt over a big field, and strange it was to see all that earthly and rosy glow of fire and rolling smoke under the pale and arctic splendors of the sky. / Redwinged blackbirds have returned, to the alder swamp, and I have seen a few grackles. Last year a great flock of grackles pulled up every bit of sweet corn from a neighbor's kitchen garden. / Mudtime continues, and I hear of people getting stuck on the way to town meeting. By dint of careful driving and sound good judgment, my friend Willard Pinkham who handles our R.F.D. gets to the farm, and glad we are to see him. / Elizabeth, who has just been out for a walk, says that there is a patch of snow to the northwest of the lilac bushes, but that the buds are showing signs of life.

There is one principle which our world would do well to remember, for it is of first importance whether one sharpens a pencil, builds a house, bakes bread, or lays the intended foundations for Utopia. It is this — that what we make is conditioned by the means we use making it. We may have the best intentions in the world, but if we sharpen our pencils with a dull knife or build a house with a faulty rule, the pencil will be badly sharpened and the house will have an odd little way of opening doors by itself and leaning to one side.

In our barn the larger beams were worked over and squared by someone using what was probably an old-fashioned ship builder's axe. They are honestly and carefully made, and something of the humanity of the past is in them to this day. Certain other beams have been sawed out, and they are good beams, too, though quite different in look and feeling. The means used in making have marked each kind of beam for all time.

But I do not wish to labor the point. It is enough to say that prophets of expediency who are careless of the means they use and who work outside the human and moral values, have never been able to build anything humanly worth while.

XVI

All day long the whole neighborhood has been watching the ice go out. For about a week now, it has been getting ready to go, its pools of open water lengthening to the south of islands and southward-facing promontories. The open bay which has been in existence for a fortnight by the old mill to the south has been clearly growing larger, the dark pond water surfaced with sunshine and the reflected blue of the spring sky.

Everything would now depend on a turn of the wind, said the farmers. On "the neck" we share a common store of knowledge about the pond; we know when it has been high and when it has been low, and there are some among us who can recall what more than eighty springs have done to the ice. This year it looked like an early clearing. Four days of warm, even of hot weather had been at work on that worn, rain-colored flatness now turned rain-color and blue. This morning the northwest wind carried the day.

From farm windows looking down to the opening waters over kitchen sinks, from clotheslines where the northwest wind billowed the farm shirts, the overalls, and the underwear, the women took time to glance thoughtfully down.

All the men, too, were watching the familiar scene from a corner of their eye, pausing as they went across high ground to study the look of the pond and the enlarging pools. The great floor of winter was breaking up.

The open water by the islands and the promontories had spread, cracks and channels had appeared, and detached floes were slowly, very slowly drifting southerly. Larger islands of ice were breaking from the northerly mass and floating off into the southern reaches of the pond, which thus opened northward against the warm and pleasant wind. Yet far to the north I could see a floor of ice apparently only just beginning to feel the power of the wind and the hot sun.

By three o'clock in the afternoon, our region of the pond had entirely cleared. True, there was still ice on the shore, frozen even under a hot sun to the rocks and gravels it had overlain all winter long, and the west wind had blown some ice into shallow coves on the southeast side, but all else was the blue and living water of the living and awakened year. Three or four small ice cakes twinkling in the afternoon light only heightened the sense of summer by their dramatic contrast with the genial temper of the day.

In a few hours, the landscape had burned one of the great corners of the year. It was a different world, now, a world out of chains, and for the first time one could see in Nature that caprice of liberated motion which is the seal of summer and its rich and wayward being.

Moods and fantasies of earth, unseen for almost six months, had come with magical swiftness into their renewed and seasonal existence. Once more the dark wind rushed before me down the slope and out on the open water, once more the catspaws of wind formed twinkling on the surface of the cove, lingered their strange moment and were gone. A whole new pattern of light and wonder has become a part of life. There was something else; what was it? Suddenly I had the answer: it was the smell of fresh water, the pond smell, touching a familiar chord of country memory.

FARM DIARY

On the way to Linwood Palmer's grocery, I note a neighbor planting peas. The well-drained, hilltop land looked about ready, and the soil had been well prepared. / Tomato seedlings are now a part of every farm kitchen, standing in the window "which gets the most sun." The "Marglobe" tomato is rather a favorite of mine. / A friend tells me that European governments are sending men over here to study contour farming. / An old farm which was bought recently after having been untenanted for years has been burned flat. My friend, John Buchan, who was to repair the chimney, now wonders what is the proper thing to do about the key? He had it from the new owner, and it was a mishap of the new owner which started the fire. / The seacoast being clear of ice and the coastal roads free at last of mudtime, we have our first visitors from saltwater. Out of an aged coupe step two men dressed not like farmers but like fishermen and wearing folded-down rubber boots. A father and a grown son, both lean, salty, and blue-eyed. We buy some fine clams, and I promise a chowder for supper. The men are often the chowder makers here. My friend and fellow Grange member Jack Burns made the Grange a wonderful clam chowder for installation night. / Elizabeth, who likes lilies, wants me to put in some hardy types here and there by the stone walls.

On a dark and none too warm evening, the alder swamp rings with the triumphant chorus of a whole nation of spring peepers. The living, exultant noise sounds like a frenzy of tiny sleighbells, and through it one hears the musical trilling of the common toad, and the occasional jug-o-rum of a bull frog. Heard nearby, the din from the swamp is almost deafening. It is a Dionysian ecstasy of night and spring, a shouting and a rejoicing out of puddles and streams, a festival of belief in sheer animal existence.

What has come over man that he has so lost this animal faith? If he wishes to stay alive as a creature of earth, it is to this faith that he must cling at all possible cost, for let him once relax his hold, out of his own being will emerge that brood of pessimisms and despairs which will bend back his fingers till they have broken his hold on life, and with it his vital and primitive strength. The body is not all of us, though a metaphorical animal carries us all upon its back, and even as the body keeps its own mysterious wills — even such as that of the heart to beat — so must it have its own appropriate and earthly faith. It was a fine music from the marsh, and in these our times I wish that all the world had been there to hear.

XVII

The farm landscape remains winterish and rather grim though today's south wind has a real warmth in it, and the pond is now free of ice. A remnant of the ice, I note, is still visible this morning lying crumpled upon itself along the opposite shore. Now that the pond is open, however, and the expanse of bright blue water twinkles in the sunshine of a bright blue day, none of us feels that spring can be far behind.

Wondering what the pond edge would have to show a day after the vernal clearing, I went walking yesterday afternoon along our own west shore, making a rather muddy pilgrimage down the sodden fields to the tumbled and stony margin of my land. Though the pond has its sandy beaches we are not fortunate enough to possess one, and our shore is the usual glacial conglomeration and disorder of stones and small boulders sloping down from the turf into the three and four feet of water just off-shore.

The water was high, the wavelets tumbling in over the drowned stones to strike the higher rocks and the sod of the field, and the miniature waves, as they hastened shorewards, were as diamond clear as the waters of a spring. What touches the heart most deeply, perhaps, was the new sense of freedom and motion which had come into being in a world which only two days ago had been sealed up in a steely-blackish prison of rotten ice. Now all this aspect of nature was alive again, the small freshwater waves rolling in upon their chaos of cold, greyish stones and flinging up as they struck heavy, rounded, crystal-clear drops of living water. The air was full of small plashing noises and watery chuckles whose pleasant and incessant chatter rose from the rock-marge to form a kind of obligato to the sound of a light southwest wind in the porches of the ears. Looking directly down into the water, I could see that the sunlight passing through the moving wavelets made dissolving patterns of light on the submerged stones, the light itself moving shoreward in tiny gleams and speckles of watery sunshine which had their instant of being and then were gone.

I could see no fish but it came to my mind that our local fishermen would all be anxious to try their luck now that the ice was out. They like to bring home one of the small salmon with which the state stocked these waters some years ago, though the pond is really famous for its native, small-mouthed bass. Such a fish, caught and dressed in the evening, the steel knives busy above a newspaper in the kitchen sink, certainly makes a wonderful farm breakfast! I have often had young bass swim around my toes when I myself went swimming, but this time the clear water was empty of life of any kind.

Trudging homeward to the red farm above the slope, I noticed something which gave me a real sense of seasonal hope. The clouds moving northerly on the unusually warm south wind had for the first time this year a summer look and a summer character. The earth below, it is true, remained rather winterish and pale, but above the pines, in the day's mild sky, summer itself went sailing past. Later in the afternoon, as if to fill in the picture, a robin gave us a first song — well, not a song, perhaps, but a cheerful and musical warble, and this was the first bird music I had chanced to hear.

FARM DIARY

The warm day closes with a thunderstorm to the "suth'ard," the lightning being unusually yellow in color, and making a yellow flare behind the wintry trees. / At supper, Elizabeth says that she hopes I will be sure to order seed for a row of sunflowers. She prefers the familiar, old-fashioned kind to the new decorative hybrids. / First loons calling from the pond, the wild, beautiful, ululating cry rising from somewhere in the dark of the open waters. / New growth in last year's ploughed land already a faint, rather pale green. / The birds begin to arrive, tree swallows on April ninth, fox sparrows on the tenth, and a first marsh hawk appears on the eleventh and hunts the fields through a light fall of snow. / Ellis Simmons, who lived with us here two years, returns to give me a day's work, and we have a fine out o'door session cleaning up after winter, and thinning out a copse of saplings near the pond. / More bronze grackles, a thoroughly unpopular bird in the farm country. Nobody here has a good word to say for them. / The coal fire made the house so uncomfortably hot on the warm day that I am letting it go out and changing over to wood. / Quiet and solitary evening, and I spend a pleasant half hour in the kitchen rocking chair going through nursery catalogues to see if some eastern grower offers the Haralson apple. I hear good things of it from friends in the west.

There are times when I wish that the word "hero" might again claim the honor once its due. In our age it has become so vulgarized and cheapened that the meaning has gone out of it. In the classical past, it seems to have been applied to those figures of mythology and shadowy history who, being men in semblance and living in a human world, contrived somehow to be more than men; doers of adventurous deeds "on the side of life" like Hercules and Perseus or Hector of the walls of Troy. What can be done to rescue so honorable a word from the street?

For my own part, whenever I think of the word "hero," I think of those United States Army privates who more than a generation ago allowed themselves to be used as "human guinea pigs," in establishing the mosquito theory of the cause of that foul and malignant disease, yellow fever. That act was heroism in the great sense of a great word, and these men were "heroes" if man has ever produced heroes. It is good to remember that a group of rather humble young Americans made this superb gesture.

XVIII

A spell of cold and rainy weather from the North Atlantic drifts inland across the drenched and cheerless coast; thin fog blurs the distant reaches of the pond, and a light wind which never dies down blows sudden drizzles of rain against the windows to the east. It is a day for a huge, reassuring open fire, but our kitchen fireplace being still blocked with its fire front and the winter stove, we have had to content ourselves with keeping a good fire burning in the range. The successive showers are almost soundless, but I am aware of them as they come because with each arrival the tinkle of the cistern in-flow grows louder under the boards of the kitchen floor. The only other real sound is that of the kettle beginning a humming sigh from the back of the range, a mild, contented, and indoor music very appropriate to the day.

As I write, the kitchen clock tells me that it is the middle of the afternoon, and presently comes rain in a real shower. Though I have been held back all day from various tasks outside, I find my mind content to stay under a roof on so cheerless an afternoon. It is on such a day that one comes to feel and appreciate the personality of one's house, and that "the house spirit," as the Chinese say, seems in a mood to tell what it has to tell. If the house is an old one, and has been cherished, a real sense of the past comes to life within the walls and the window panes. A hundred and twenty-five years have passed like cloud shadows over this roof since young men raised the timber above the field stone cellars and the boulders at the corners, for well over a hundred years the touch of human life has smoothed the house as the flowing of a brook wears smooth a pebble in the current of the stream. Every outer threshold, for instance, shows the scooped hollow of the footsteps of those who have come and gone down the archways of the years.

Elizabeth says, "Say of it first that it is a kind house." There are no places which catch and trip the passerby, no beams or corners which bump unwary heads, no latches or gadgets which pinch the fingers. It has no architectural malices which lie in wait.

It is perhaps in the kitchen that one is most aware of the human past, for the kitchen, even as it is now, was the center of existence of the farm. In this room and before the great fireplace assembled the young married men who cleared the land and the first fields, the men and their sons who cleared the larger fields and the pasture hill, the countrymen who shaped the fine timbers of the team with the ship builders' axe, and the women of the farm who did the cooking, the weaving, the knitting, and kept the household together. They must have been a hardy lot to have stood these winters without stoves. Wheat flour was scarce in the frontier north in those ancient days, and neighbors tell me that it was barley bread and rye bread and coin-cake which were baked in the brick ovens and in the iron skillets to one side of the living fire.

I once had a glimpse of the room as it might have been in the early nineteenth century. There had come to work with us a young Passamaquoddy Indian, and it came about that one October night we left the farm in his care and went forth to have supper with friends. The boy could neither read nor write, and when his work was done, he simply relaxed in a rocking chair and took things in a kind of restful blank.

When we returned a little before eleven, I noticed as we drove in that the lamps in the kitchen had all been turned very low. Where was Roland, for that was our Indian's very un-Indian name? Entering the kitchen quietly, we came upon a scene the farm will long remember. The boy had taken an old blanket from his bed, rolled up in it, stretched himself longwise on the floor before the dying fire, and gone to sleep. Even thus his Indian ancestors had made themselves at home at some colonial neighbor's. The old Yankee kitchen, the darkness, and the drowsy fire, the tanned out-of-door young face — it was the past and pure romance. I hated to wake him, but I did so, and with the ceremonious politeness which was a part of his spirit, he took his candle, said a proper good night, and went to bed. I wish I knew what has become of him. Wherever he is, the farm wishes him well.

FARM DIARY

May Day, and an icy wind from the north together with a grey drizzle of rain. Not a day for May baskets and merrymaking, but a time for the warm kitchen and the fortifying strength of a good, hot breakfast. / "Hope springs eternal in the human breast," and once again I am setting out a pair of quince trees. The quince does not thrive in our northerly world, though I am told that in the milder climate south of Portland the tree is sometimes seen on old farms. The quince is not rare south of Boston, and it flourishes on Cape Cod. In southern Europe baked quinces are served as we serve baked apples, and they are particularly good. Our word "marmalade" originally meant a quince preserve. / The high prices of things are more than ever forcing the farms back on their own resources. Winter clothes which can be made to go another season will all be neatly and strongly repaired, and I am following suit in having the elbows of my favorite winter jacket patched with pliable leather. / Maurice Day tells me of having recently gone to a "pie supper" served at the close of a Grange entertainment, the tables being spread from end to end with an incomparble variety and splendor of all kinds of pie, nothing but pie. Sounds full of interest. / Fell asleep listening to a murmur of rain, first having put a stick of oak on the bedroom fire.

In spite of rain and cloud, the spring draws near. In the wet and dripping trees, even on these forlorn afternoons, the robins have managed the beginnings of a song. With the change, there comes something particularly needed by the human spirit — an affirmation of that eternal change in nature which rules out stagnancy, and the appearance of the entirely new within the pattern of the old. We are not treated to fantasies and monsters; the world remains the world we have known. I suspect that in human existence our problem is the finding of some like harmony between what is fixed and of the pattern and what is untried and eager to be born.

XIX

When it comes to pass in the country that we must leave our houses alone and empty by night in order to attend some village festivity, we all of us do so more or less unwillingly. To leave the farm untended and unwatched, even for a moment, goes against the grain, and where the neighbors have children of a competent age, farm households often work out some arrangement whereby the youngsters will take their school books with them to the house, and study there at the kitchen table until the farm family returns before the clock has ticked away too many hours. This kind of neighborly help is much appreciated in winter time, when the visitors not only keep an eye on things in general but also put wood on the kitchen fire. Many a time I have seen the oilcloth of such a table scattered over with sheets of arithmetic paper and village school books, and found somebody's youngsters standing up by their chairs waiting for their small reward and ready to be taken home.

When there are no neighbors handy, there is nothing one can do but abandon the house to its loneliness. A profound instinct then sends us through the house to check every fire, to blow out every lamp, and figuratively to look into every corner. If we are satisfied, out we go, closing the door behind us on the warm, empty, and forsaken darkness within, and trusting all will be in proper order when we return. Few of us lock the door.

It was after eleven when I reached the farm last night after having been to a Grange meeting with my kind neighbors, Carroll and Louise. Knowing that it would be pitch dark when we returned, I carried with me to their farm a lantern to light me home. The old-fashioned lantern is our traveling light here, and on winter nights when we hear the voices of visitors outside, we look from the window to see a yellow lantern light moving towards us across the snow. Flashlights are creeping in, being enormously convenient, but the cheerful lighted lantern is what we really like. Having arrived at Carroll and Louise's, I blew out the flame and stood the lantern on the kitchen table to await my home coming. When their farm had been put in order, and the cat turned out into the shed, we all got into Carroll's truck and drove off to the village and the meeting.

It was a pleasant session, and friendly with the natural friendliness of a neighborhood gathering united in a common aim. Our Grange, moreover, accomplishes something whose importance is often overlooked in America; it mingles together in a social goodtime the elderly, the middle-aged, and the young of a community. The various generations, in our republic, tend to live far too much to themselves.

The meeting at an end, and a sort of cheerful picnic meal consumed, people began to say goodby, and presently Carroll drove us home down the country roads. Once we had reached his farm, I myself said goodnight, lit my lantern, and struck out for the farm.

As I walked ahead into the country silence with the pond to my right and the pine forest to my left across the upper field, I began to see how summer had rolled back into the sky. So early had I been going to bed that I had not been aware of the great change in the heavens. The winter constellations had vanished in the west, sinking into the clear, luminous sky beyond the dark of the woods, and out of the east had rolled the thinner-strewn summer signs and starry fig-ures. Dominant in the starry depth of the abyss and giving particular beauty to the night, the no-ble planet Jupiter hung aloft as lord of the spring, his golden lamp just beyond the reach of the bright claws of the Scorpion. Putting down my lantern awhile, and pausing to stare and listen, I could hear from far away the tiny, exultant bells of the spring-peepers in the marsh.

How still was the red house and empty the stare of the unlighted windows! Opening the door into its lingering warmth, I walked quickly to the kitchen range, and put a few pieces of dry wood on the glowing ashes of the fire.

A warm rain of the kind some call "a growing rain" comes with a S.W. wind, and in the bright sunshine of the next morning I notice that the grass looks greener than ever and that the apple tree buds are preparing to open. / Another warm day with vapor masses drifting in from seaward, and the roads now being passable, the first country trading wagon comes to the door. The driver, a lean grey-haired man of middle age, very neatly dressed in out o'door country clothes, looks like a retired school principal, and for all I know, may be one, as in this region people like to have something to do once they settle down. He comes into the kitchen carrying a big market basket full of everything from shaving soaps to tins of kitchen spices. I buy an assortment of household needs; we talk a little, and away he goes. / Glad to see that the perennials Elizabeth planted last season have apparently come through the winter unusually well. / A fisherman friend from one of the outer islands, a husky youngster in blue civilian pants, a Navy seajacket, and a peaked cap, hails me on the street in Damariscotta and we discuss the approaching arrival of those small land birds who — to some extent — travel by sea. Rather surprisingly, the prize seafarer here is the ruby-throated humming bird, and the fishermen often tell me of seeing humming birds far out on Penobscot Bay.

Some of the religions have outspokenly taught the depravity of man, others have insisted on a rather sugary natural goodness. I hold to neither extreme. Save for those tragic individuals whom something physiological or mental twists towards what is wrong, I have always thought that people, on the whole, are as good as they are able to be. As they are able to be — that is the point, and if such is the natural direction, there is surely something very touching and decent in our troubled race. What is clear is that we simply cannot get on without giving the inclination a chance and providing it with some definite pattern and teaching of morality.

XX

With the arrival of warmth and the wayward genialities of our northern spring, something returns to the farm which is rather a rarity here in the really cold winter — the presence and mystery of rain. Again and again, when weather reports indicate rain scarce a hundred miles away to the south and west, what we get is the same storm as driving snow.

An old friend in the village, a careful observer, tells me that the snow often begins to fall just as the tide reaches the flood. In comes the cold northern sea under the threatening day, filling the estuaries and over-running the tidal flats with its deep and powerful streams, and then — out of the greyness comes the snow. Sometimes the flood, the snow, and the night arrive together, and we bring in more wood, and look to a white world in the morning.

Now, however, the earth leans towards the sun, and what we get is rain. It is spring rain, and so far we have had no drenching, day-long downpours of it, but only scattered showers from a sky whose monotony of rain and grey has been wan with light.

It is such a drizzle as I write, and I can hear the

familiar sound of which I have already spoken, the murmur and tinkle of the rainwater falling into the cistern below the kitchen floor. Spatters of rain stand on the western windows, and outside goes on the long, steady, life-giving drenching of the earth. On the pasture rocks, it will be falling through the pines at the circumference, and soaking everywhere into the brown, needle-covered ground; in the hemlocks, it will be dripping from the greenery above down upon delicate twigs which will nod an instant like things poised on a delicate wire; here and there, all through the wood, the little rain brooks will be foamily chattering as they run through their familiar channels in and out of the mossy and tumbled stones. The strange sigh, the grave and hissing whisper of an evergreen forest in the rain will be everywhere in the air for the listening ear.

For me, it means rubber boots, an old rubber coat with a bad tear in it, and a fisherman's "souwester" I bought long ago on Matinicus Island. I have just been out to get a pail of spring water, and have splashed a little on the kitchen floor.

The outer world was full of rain and nothing else. I couldn't see a soul anywhere. No one about, no one rubber-booting it across a field, no one in sight in any farm yard, and the empty pond just a vast puddle of greyness and rain. At the end of the shed, a waterspout gurgled foolishly, whilst the leaning water in my rain barrel overflowed silently to one side. From the grass at my feet, from the fields, from the hollow of space itself, I could hear the myriad sound of the light rain and the passive and awakening land.

I have a notion that when this stops, we are going to have a week of warm winds and the good, warm, blessed sun.

FARM DIARY

Some years ago at a neighborhood auction I bought an old copy in colors of Landseer's "The Rescue," an academy picture of the 1870's. It is a "story picture" showing a defile of the Great St. Bernard pass and a young traveler lying there half-buried and unconscious in the snow. Two St. Bernard dogs have just discovered him. One, whom we call "the nurse," is attempting to rouse the youth whilst the other, whom we call "the doctor," is giving tongue in a noble pose, and pawing away the drifts. The "doctor" has a blanket wound about his middle and the famous keg of brandy suspended from his collar. In the wild, Alpine background some monks of St. Bernard are hastening to the scene. This picture marks winter for us at the farm. It goes up on the kitchen wall the day the first snow falls, and I take it down the day the ice goes out of the pond. Every farm and every family ought to have a few ritual jokes that are all their own. / The first fruits of the northern year, rhubarb stalks, are coming along. The farm will have to manage a small rhubarb pie somehow or other, or the season won't begin in proper style.

It often strikes me that in our modern Babylons you never see anything begin. Everything comes to you, even thought, at a certain stage of its development, like an iceberg lettuce. Now life is more a matter of beginnings than of endings, and without some sense of the beginning of things, there is no proper perspective on the whole mystery of living. This is only one detail, but it will serve as one of the marks of the whole incomplete urban perspective in which we live. For the city governs us now as never before; it tells us what to love and what to hate, what to believe and what not to believe, and even what to make of human nature.

I begin to suspect that we should be more on our guard against Babylon when its urbanism has gone bloodless and sterile, and it insists on our taking its false maps of the human adventure. We must regain the truer and fuller perspective, one leading back to origins and to beginnings human, earthy, concealed, and slow. No map is worthy a penny which does not include both the city and the fields.

XXI

All morning long the farm has been in a fine, cheerful, and uproarious confusion. Our friend Louis French the plumber having come to help us, we have been changing over the kitchens, connecting our water system, tuning-up gas engines, and redistributing the furniture. Out went the winter stove and off came the storm shutters, and while we men folk were going upstairs and downstairs checking for leaks and turning on sputtering faucets, Elizabeth and our kind neighbor Barbara Oliver were hunting the winter out of his last hiding places in the closed bedrooms, and putting him to flight through the great front door. It was hard physical work for all of us, but now that the place is in order again, the house positively glows with a vernal and country satisfaction.

To explain the turmoil, I had best make clear the summer and winter ritual of the house. Like many of these older farms, we have two kitchens in the ell, a summer one and a winter one, each with its own sink, its chimney, and its running water. Of the two, the "summer kitchen" is the cooler and more airy, and in some ways the easier to use. It is a pleasant room with painted white walls, pearl-grey woodwork, old beams left "natural" and a brown linoleum floor. We sometimes call it the "St. Lawrence kitchen" because some of the old-fashioned jars and containers were picked up by Elizabeth in the river villages.

The "winter kitchen" is the room we turn to when the late autumnal cold begins to close in upon the house. This is the room which is our final stronghold against the snow. It is warmer than its summer counterpart and nearer the main house, and there is a sort of primitive cellar lurking beneath the floor. A huge red brick chimney fireplace built out into the room is here the center of life, cheerful all autumn long with hardwood fires. Unwilling as we are to close it off, there is always some November day when we seal the fireplace cave with a "fire-front," and set up an old winter stove we store in a corner of the shed. The summer kitchen is then drained, the last fire suffered to go out, the pots and pans transferred, and the room abandoned to the cold. Beyond the partition, the pail from the spring becomes our drinking water, the cistern supply our washing water, and the winter range our household deity.

It was on this winter economy we descended this morning a vernal wolf on the fold. Lawrence and I worked at the house, the plumber and his helper at the lake, and in an hour or two we had the lake water up the hill and humming in the pipes, and the engine going and the great cypress tank overflowing like water over a dam. The familiar clank of the cistern pump would be heard no more awhile. The next thing on the program was the summer kitchen, and here the ladies came to our aid, abandoning whatever they were up to in the front of the house. In three shakes of a lamb's tail, or so it seemed, they had it in proper order, its pots and pans hung on the wall, a fire burning in the range, and a kettle steaming.

Only one last thing remained to be done, the moving out of the winter stove. We had built but a small fire in it that morning, and this was now only a bed of ash. Elizabeth says that we all went for it in a kind of "solemn rush." It is not a heavy stove, and surrounded by plumbers and by Lawrence and myself, it went very peaceably into the shed. An easy tug at the fire-front, and there stood the fireplace yawning black, and looking rather sooty and in need of sweeping. I made this my job and, when I had finished, Lawrence drove us all forth and took a pail and mop and did the floor. Tonight, if it is cool, Elizabeth will light the first fire for it is one of my pet superstitions, inherited from a wise and ever-honored grandmother, that the first hearthfire of the year must be lit by the woman of the house.

The winter kitchen now looked very large. Its windows were open, and all the pleasant world outside seemed full of the singing of birds. Summer was at hand, the trees were in young leaf, the fields were really green, and the skies were mild and blue. In the house, too, it was summer again. Musing a moment on the change, there came to me out of the long past a pretty song taught me in childhood from a songbook of all nations, "Winter farewell, winter farewell, and away you go and trouble us no more."

FARM DIARY

Friends tell me that flocks of Canada geese are still in the rivers and saltwater estuaries, not having yet left us for the higher north. / And the chipping sparrows are back, familiars of the farmhouse and the lawn, great hunters of crumbs and the small ants who go to and fro on the piazza. / People who are connected with the "tourist trade" are now busy everywhere, giving final touches to their cabins and rooms, and putting up road signs brightened with fresh paint. / Our winter woolens now vanish into attic bureaus and cedar chests, and out come the blue denims and the mended cotton shirts and the battered straw hats. / Great plans and confabs in the fireplace kitchen concerned with another vast planting of potatoes. / When the season opens on June first, I guess I'll try and see if I can't get us a nice bass for a farm breakfast.

Our neighbors, the Olivers, have given Elizabeth a birthday present of a handloomed towel made at their farm some seventy years ago. Elwell Oliver tells me that it was woven by his mother, who was famous for her fine weaving, and that the flax of which it is made was both grown and spun here by the shores of the pond. What has this memorial of the handicrafts which something made by the machine does not possess? The answer can be given in a phrase; it has life. The machine-made thing has the mark of the un-living device. The thing made by hand has the signature of the living spirit.

XXII

This morning Irving Oliver came over to plough the kitchen garden by the barn. He brought with him the rig he uses, a sulky-plough pulled by his cherished team of huge white horses, the inseparable, good-tempered, and willing Major and Prince. Irving believes, and he is entirely right, that it is a waste of time and money to fool with expensive machinery for our kind of farming. When he came driving towards us, coming over the fields from another neighbor's, it was certainly a sight to cheer the country heart! The sulky-plough looked like a Roman chariot, no less, with its fine matched pair pulling confidently forward, their great equine heads held boldly up, and their manes stirring with the motion forward and a touch of the southwest wind.

When one's country lies under the snow for months of the year, and the spring which isn't quite a spring comes but a step or two ahead of summer, the first ploughing of one's land can be something to stir the heart. On came Irving in his chariot, the iron wheels rolling out their iron sound as they reached the harder ground leading to the barn, and presently Major and Prince were there beside us, and Irving holding the reins in his hand, and asking me just what I wanted done.

Irving is an old friend and neighbor, and one of the best. He is still in his thirties, a young family man, lean, strong, and grey-eyed. We passed the time of day, neighbor fashion, and then got down to business.

"You want this piece ploughed the same size as last year?" "Bout the same, but give me five more furrows towards the pond."

The horses stirred, lifting their huge deliberate feet and shifting their vast selves over; down went a blade, took hold, and the first wave of earth began to roll over and glisten in the light. Our soil is heavy, and the clays and pale, northern gravels of the glaciers are consolidated in it with what there is of top soil, humus and the fertility of a hundred and fifty successive years of barn manure. A few black flies, occasional nuisances of warm days in mid-May, once in a while demanded a brush of the hands but no one paid any real attention to them, and Major and Prince seemed entirely undisturbed. Perhaps the tree swallows were giving us help, for their shadows passed and repassed over the furrows in the warm and pleasant sun.

A sulky-plough is a particularly good rig for our kind of soil and these old-fashioned fields, and Irving handles it and his fine team with sureness and skill. The great creatures ploughed with an animal goodwill, with a kind of honest and confident assurance that all was well in their

111

equine world; one could see that they were as much at ease with Irving as Irving was with them. He has always taken pride in their handsome appearance, and in their powers.

Over and over rolled the waves of soil, stray tufts of grass and precocious weeds tumbling under the long volutes of the furrows, whilst the glisten of earth curled over above, revealing the deeper clays, the small embedded stones, and the pink of earthworms disturbed in their fertile tunnels underground. Beyond the ploughing and down the slopes, the pond lay blue and still, whilst overhead the sun in the south drew near the heights of noon.

The living year had begun.

FARM DIARY

Sign of the times . . . an out-of-state car driven by a decent stranger in his early forties drives in, and I am asked if I know where one can buy a farm? I give him an agent's address, and away he goes. / The animal life of the hayfields is again coming into being. Going down to the pump at the pond, small leopard-frogs now scramble out from before my feet here and there along the path. / Our first show of wild flowers has begun, and the familiar carpets of bluets or "Quaker Ladies" are in bloom on damp hillsides and in old, wet grassland still open in the woods. / Have been putting in some strawberry plants of a trick variety which does not develop runners. Our cold springs here are not friendly to strawberries, and I am always trying experiments. These plants came from Iowa, and arrived in excellent condition. / Elizabeth has returned from a visit, bringing the house a present of a handwoven tablecloth from some old Mennonite farm in Pennsylvania. Looks to me like work of the 1870's. The design is a simple blue and white check. A beautiful, human, and honest thing, and peace be with the hands that made it.

I have been sitting in a farm kitchen, holding down a rocking chair in an impromptu gathering of friends and neighbors, and what I now remember is how uproariously we all laughed together over any number of things.

I have only a hazy notion as to what so amused me, for on such an evening the whole remembered humor of the countryside blows through the room and the mind, keeping the sense of place vigorously alive and helping us laugh at ourselves and with ourselves. One hears of the picturesque characters, the absurd adventures, the comic predicaments, the drolleries of animals — everything which has been cherished by a people with a very lively and kindly sense of fun.

Are we farm people the only ones left who still laugh with gusto in the old, almost roll-on-the-floor way? I sometimes rather fear so. On the farms we laugh, I think, from the body and the human spirit whilst the age, if it laughs at all, screams from a tension of the nerves. Heaven knows that the times have little to laugh at, though would they had, for laughter is a notable part of our humanity, a thing seemingly given to man alone.

When it thins down into the trickle of the wisecrack and the sneer, the sense of proportion is gone. I am glad we laughed as we did. The devilry of this world is the work of the too serious. I walked home still merry, down the dark road alongside a great planet rising in the east.

XXIII

I have just returned from a visit to Damariscotta Mills and the alewife run. Every year we all go over to see this great run of fish which is one of the marvels of our coast.

Some three miles away as the crow flies, the long, narrow arm of our pond flows south to a natural dam some fifty feet high, and there winds and tumbles down a stairway of cascades into the salt water of a tidal bay. The glen of the cascades is such a scene as one might find in an old Currier and Ives print or imagine for oneself out of Thoreau's America — a glen, a vale, of old rocks and tall, peaceful elms, of the incessant sound of waterfalls, and the white wings of seagulls coming and going, going and coming, far above and in the blue. Old houses have closed in to one side, their shingles forever wet with spray where they stand above the water, and the open windows of their kitchens and sheds forever full of the beautiful, incessant sound of the pouting streams.

It is to these waters that the alewives come every spring, going up to the pond to spawn from their unknown winter refuge in the outer sea. Though we call such runs here "herring runs," the fish is not a true herring though it resembles one in size and shape. Our word "alewife" is a sort of early colonial transformation into English sound of an Indian word used by the redmen of seventeenth-century Massachusetts, and carried downeast by early settlers of our towns.

Perhaps a million or so fish crowd and swarm into the bay. They arrive in April, and their presence in the salt river is signalled to us by a simultaneous arrival of fishing birds from all our region of the coast. The gulls come, a cloud of wings and hungry cries, the fierce osprey finds himself a shelter and a watch-tower and the fiercer and piratic eagle comes to take the osprey's catch. The fish show no haste in going up into the pond. The living mass waits for good weather, and for a new warmth in the outlet stream. On some fine morning in May, with the sun shining overhead, the run begins.

Entering from the bay, the thickly-crowding, blue-backed, golden-bellied masses are confronted by a channel which branches at the dam into two wild, outrushing brooks. One stream leads to the cascades and to wooden basins from which the alewives are dipped in nets and sent to the smokehouse, for there is an ancient commerce in these fish between our villages and the West Indian isles. It is probably the last relic of the eighteenth-century economy of colonial America. The other stream leads to a winding stair of old fieldstone basins built well over a hundred years ago to help the run move up into the pond.

Built as ruggedly as our boulder walls, and mellowed now by water and the years, these basins on the slope interpose their twistings and turnings to the furious descent of one branch of the outlet stream and at the top lead out of crying foam and currents into the mild and quiet haven of the pond.

The day being warm and summerish and the tide high in the morning, there was a fine run moving upstream when I arrived. One could see the unnumbered mass moving in from the bay, and holding its own in the strong current of fresh water, a stream of life battling an opposing stream. There was a touch of lavender in the blue-black color of the massed fish as they swam under the skin of the brown and rippled water, the swarm pressing close together, each fish having just room to move its fins and no more.

Above and in the channel of the basins the stream was all a miracle of water and life, of life pressing onward, struggling fiercely to turn, climbing, climbing through the wild watery roar and the torrent whose foam was swift with the shadow and sunlight of the elms overhead, life pressing on, believing in itself, keeping the first faith, and remembering the immemorial decree.

FARM DIARY

A household catastrophe. While rummaging

117

about on the kitchen table, I knock over my bottle of ink and spill a great, black puddle on the Mennonite tablecloth. Household remedies come quickly into play, a rinsing, a twenty-four hour soaking in sour milk, and a last treatment with salt and lemon juice. Our kind friend Mrs. Linwood Palmer tells Elizabeth to be sure to use the lemon and salt treatment in full sunlight. Presto change-o! All well again, and you'd never know that anything had happened. / The gasoline pump at the pond having developed a cussedness of being slow to start, my new neighbor Freddy French, late First Sergeant USA, comes over to give me a friendly and much appreciated lift, and soon has the engine going in good style. / Weather bureau warning of a cold night and a possible frost, and the whole neighborhood in a rush to cover what tomatoes have been hazarded outdoors. Temperature at one A.M., 36.

Among the many things for which I remain profoundly grateful is the fact that so much of life defies human explanation. The unimaginative and the dull may insist that they have an explanation for everything, and level at every wonder and mystery of life their popgun theories, but God be praised, their wooden guns have not yet dislodged the smallest star. It is well that this be so, for the human spirit can die of explanations, even if, like many modern formulae,

118

they are but explanations which do not explain.

A world without wonder, and a way of mind without wonder, becomes a world without imagination, and without imagination man is a poor and stunted creature. Religion, poetry, and all the arts have their sources in this upwelling of wonder and surprise. Let us thank God that so much will forever remain out of reach, safe from our inquiry, inviolate forever from our touch.

XXIV

It is summer at last, and the world is alive again in the warm and pleasant air. Tree leaves are not yet fully out, but branches are again clothed in green, and once again do shadows of summer move with swaying bough and twig across the rustic unevenness of the farmhouse lawn. Within the earth, upon it, and above it, life stirs and would go on. All day long our flowering apples hum with the sound of honey bees, and late into the dusk one huge bumble bee prolongs the drowsy murmur, working at the top of the tree where the flowers catch the very last of the evening light.

Perhaps in all our country scene, nothing seems more eager and living than the birds. Because this is old forest country only here and there opened into farms, we have a rather large variety of species. Among them are birds of the northern woods, birds of the farm country, birds who like pond shores, water birds, and even strays from the neighboring Atlantic. You never can tell what you may see. Two years ago, for instance, that fantastic creature, the northern pileated woodpecker flew out of the woods and rested for awhile on the ridge pole of our disused icehouse, and only last fall, going down to the fields after a wild northeaster, I startled up a red-legged guillemot from between the blown, dishevelled rows of corn. It was a strange sight to see that ocean creature flying through inland Maine.

Certain birds we can count on as familiars. Robins are our songsters, cheerfully loquacious and musically talkative from the nearer trees, sociable heralds of the early light, and builders of nests in absurd places. Last year a robin who would have had difficulties with an intelligence test, built a nest under the big tank on a beam exposed to the deluges of the frequent overflows. The farm wondered if she planned to raise ducks! Chimney swifts have built in the chimney of my bedroom, and sometimes wake me in the early morning with the muffled and hollow roaring of their wings as they flutter up from their cavern of night and soot into the air of dawn.

The usual yellow warblers are at home in a sheltered apple tree whose branches shade the house, the usual catbirds are in their choke-cherry thicket, and the tree swallows have again taken over the bird house which needs a coat of paint. The barn swallows, too, have come, and for the time being are hunting the air above and about the house, on tireless wings darting and glancing high above the old apple tree in flower, the red water tank, and the two tall, austere chimneys of the ell. In the quiet evenings after sundown we hear the thrushes calling from the woods.

If these are the familiars of the house, the hilltop, and the barn, the bobolink is the very spirit of the fields. These slopes rolling down to the pond are a bobolink paradise, and all summer long we live in sight and sound of them, the fields housing perhaps a dozen or even twenty pairs. The male birds arrive in the middle of May, and the females follow soon after. As my old friend Edward Forbush once wrote, "The bobolink is the harlequin of the fields, and he wears his suit wrong-side up." Again and again here, I have watched him pursue his mate, singing as he goes, the bubbling song and the purposeful, determined flight joined together in one exultant surge of living. Nests are built on the ground and are hidden with particular skill in tangles at the foot of bushy weeds and near clumps of taller grass.

The eggs once laid, the female takes charge of housekeeping, leaving the male free to celebrate his song while keeping a weather eye on the nest in case of trouble. June is our bobolink month, and it is the feast of song we are now hearing. From branches of nearby trees, from fence posts, from some swaying weed top, from the living air, the bobolink song pours downward through space like the sound of some musical waterfall. Sometimes when I am working in the kitchen garden, I lay down my trowel just to listen a while.

First bouquet of flowers on the breakfast table, a nosegay of English cowslips from the garden Elizabeth allows to run wild. This European cowslip — *Primula Officinalis* or *Veris* — does well with us, making nothing of our long winters, and welcoming the spring every year with its cheerful yellow flowers. / First summer thunderstorm of the year, and a sound of thunder in the night together with a murmur of rain and a few flares of lightning in the west. Soon over, and the house stops listening, and goes back to sleep. / The ploughing of the fields continues, and we watch Major and Prince walking to and fro, to and fro, over last year's earth, tracing furrows whose regular contour reminds me of the roll of mid-ocean waves in a light air. / Wild strawberries in bloom, the small white flowers scattered like stars in the short grass.

Under today's disorders there is something at work among the nations whose great importance has not yet been adequately realized — the need of men for a community to live in and live with. The hope is vague, unsaid, and unformulated, but the need is great, and there is something in our hearts which troubles us that we have lost what was once so beautifully called "the commonweal."

I suspect that if this open wound is to heal, it will have to heal like all wounds from the bottom, and that we shall have to begin at the beginning with the family and its obligations, with the village and its responsibilities, and with our universal and neglected duty to the earth.

XXV

High on the slope above the pond, and walled in with June grass, the corn-patch of the farm garden has been lying unplanted while waiting for warmer weather. We are so far to the north and so liable here to late frosts that early planting is a risk with such things as corn, though we plant as early as we can, well knowing that late planting brings another risk when the cold of autumn comes in a night across the hills. This year we have had rather a cold early summer, and these cold June nights have seen frosts in the lowlands of the farms. This morning, however, a change came, the sun rising hot and living over an earth already warmed with a south wind which had risen in the night.

In this northern world, a good planting day is almost a ritual accord with Nature, so much depends on it and so little time have we to lose. All up and down the farm land, we all of us went early to our work, and from my own field I could see Irving and his horses rhythmically harrowing an acre just too far away for me to hear his voice stopping and urging on his team as they walked parallel to the blue waters of the pond. Our neighbors to the south, meanwhile, had gone down to their already half-planted garden, active and busy figures working with the earth in the welcome heat and splendor of the day.

Lawrence having come to give me a hand, we got in our summer corn, both of us gratefully busy not with death but with life. Lawrence has been home about a year from the wars. He is in his later twenties, a young man of middle height and very powerfully built, and we like to have him work with us not only for his good temper but also for that serene, almost placid, quality which so often accompanies great physical strength. He has blue eyes, white teeth, and a great shock of yellow hair which, because he wears no hat, the sun burns to a kind of straw color above the healthy tan of his face.

Lawrence has long been a friend of the farm, having lived with us here in the old days, and shared the summer and the winter work and the autumn evenings by the open fire.

Working in the corn patch, the sun seemed to stand still in a sort of agricultural high noon. The earth was not hot, but warm to the touch like the side of a living animal, and growing warmer every hour as it lay basking in the sun. So warm, so radiant was the sun that there seemed no shadows on the patch in the glare of fruitful light, though in a corner the brown-paper bags of fertilizer stood hunched with a lump of shade to one side.

On the new telephone wires, a single barn swallow sat for a long while, living in his own world, and well aware of ours. We planted in rows, dropping the seed in careful spacing, Lawrence carrying an aluminum dipper he fancies and I a small lard pail which does duty every year. The patch had already been manured, a great load of old, well-seasoned barn manure having been worked in and harrowed under; dried clots and lumps of it lay dusty underfoot. One could smell the hot earth and the life within it and the sun.

Pale-yellow, wrinkled, horny, and shrunken, the corn lay in the furrows, sown on earth we had scuffed over a sprinkling of commercial. There it would awaken and rise up as corn, the truly sacred plant of America, the staff and symbol of its ancient being. The long rains would come from the east and the sea, and the black thundershowers from the west, and time and the earth would create a new thing, and the green and rustling sound of corn would be heard on the August wind.

When we had finished, we both of us washed in the shed, gratefully sluicing and soaping off field dust, sweat, and the clinging smell of fertilizer, and holding our heads beneath the plentiful warm water pouring from a tap. I had no blisters to study for it is long since I have blistered easily.

When we felt comfortable and clean, and had changed clothes in the shed chambers, we went together into the big kitchen where Elizabeth was waiting, into the pleasant room with its afternoon sunlight, its domestic order, and its sense of peace.

Have been planting some hills of "Butternut" squash, an excellent vegetable one can use from late summer on into early winter. For summer use, I like the Italian summer squash or vegetable marrow called the "Cocozelle" because it grows quickly, cooks promptly, and makes many a pleasant dish. The old-fashioned "summer squash" has never been so good since the government straightened its neck. / The farm bell having rusted up over the winter, Lawrence has taken it down to the village to be sanded and re-gilded. / Our friend Bee Day — Mrs. Maurice Day — presents us with a share of wonderful clam chowder just off the stove, and we warm it up at home, drop in the "Boston crackers" and finish it to the last potato slice and the last sublime clam.

In summer, the menfolk of our state make the best of the warm months and do the field work stripped to the waist. Long before the late, shiftless war was upon us, it was almost a state custom to work thus rigged, and one looked from the road out on what might have been an agricultural community of Fenimore Cooper Indians in blue denim pants. In our climate the fashion seems to me an excellent one, though it is per-haps not one to be followed in regions of fiercer heat and light.

The scene thus set is vigorous and alive, and there is a classical rightness to it. It is far re-moved from the idiot world of vitamin pills. The field and the workers are one; they form an earthly unity, and share together the weight of the sun and the brushing by of the wind. Our ab-stract civilization is all the poorer for having lost its sense of living by the body as well as by the brain and nerves. When it deals with the flesh, it vulgarizes it, having no sense whatever of its meaning. Perhaps it is well to remember once in a while that we were made in a human complete-ness of bone and sinew, and given the earth for our inheritance and good cheer.

XXVI

Few moments of the country year are as lovely as the green quiet of an early summer morning. Rising today soon after sunrise, I found a world as still as if the winds had not yet been created, the whole summer landscape lying immersed in quiet as in a dewy sea. Under the fresh sky and the increasing eastern light, no branch or even leaf stirred on the old apples near the door; not the smallest breath or whiplash of wandering air moved within the grass bent over and sunken down as with a weight of rain; in its hollow the pond was all one calm of peace and early morning blue. Even the young swallows on the wires, sitting as is their wont facing into the sun, kept their places and were still.

As I stood by the farm door looking down the hill slope into this world so silent and at peace, I found myself beginning to wonder about the country sounds which would presently arise to break this blessedness of quiet. Nobody as yet seemed astir; I could see no smoke as yet rising from the chimneys of the road. Suddenly across the light and silence, across space and the immense peace of the morning came a first morning sound, the crow of a rooster from some farm beyond the fields. Clear and challenging, and little muted by distance, it pierced the day — that strange and threefold outcry at once musical and harsh which is to my mind the symbol of the challenge of all things living to life itself and its possible splendors and disasters. Danger, time, the shadow of the hawk, Death itself — in that cry all were greeted and defied. And then next door I saw the smoke of a kitchen fire rising in blue unfoldings to the light.

Soon a cow lowed and another cow, breaking the quiet with that morning sound in which there is both recognition and a call for attention. Farm animals, horses in particular, are often sociable creatures, and make sociable noises and whinnyings which are greetings and little else. Half a mile down the road, my neighbor Irving Oliver's pair of white horses would now be showing a morning restlessness, and whinnying when they heard the kitchen door open and steps coming to the barn. From across the pond came the barking of a dog, but this sound was silenced almost at once, and the whole countryside returned again into its soundless peace.

The farm world, nevertheless, had begun its tasks. As I busied myself at some small chores of my own, I could see my neighbor Carroll Winchenbaugh coming and going about his barn. All up and down the country road the stoves had been lighted, the cows milked and the milk put away to cool, and breakfast made ready

131

against the cares of the day. The hens, too, had been visited and fed, all in that strange sound of cackling and crooning from the flock, and neighbors would be carrying back the two or three eggs they had happened to see, leaving the real collection till later in the morning. The frisky, crafty-eyed pig had had his "vittles," and the cats their saucer of milk beside the stove. These obligations seen to, the farm itself would presently be sitting down with a good conscience to its own repast.

The sun was rising into a sky of an even clearer blue; it promised to be a fine day. Soon one would hear the sounds of the manifold and unending work of the farm world, the sound of a farm truck, perhaps, or the noise of someone repairing and carpentering or the fine sound of a whetstone and a scythe. There would be voices in the distance across the fields, and it was almost time for the early morning train. Quiet as it remained, the day itself was coming to a new life. The heavy dew was going off into space, the pond had lost its quiescence of calm though it remained in morning peace, and a first wandering breeze, a mere sigh of the awakening air, presently fluttered the leaves of one branch of the older apple tree. The country day had begun.

FARM DIARY

Above our railroad crossing, on a wooded hillock, a number of larches stand among white pines and red. Surely one of the most beautiful greens in Nature is the green of the new leaves of this tree. / Honey bees visiting the dandelions. I see them all day long crawling over the golden faces, and filling the air with an industrious hum. / Local housewives putting up jars of dandelion greens for winter use. That green bitterness of early summer can be very refreshing when served with the potatoes and winter squash of February. / Corn beginning to show a green trace in the farm gardens, and we espy crows, those enemies who come in the quiet of the dawn. / Elizabeth meditating a day's shopping trip to Portland. / A week of northerly winds clear the sky, and cool and even cold evenings bring to a close those first early summer days.

With sundown tonight there will begin one of the great festivals of the agricultural and solar year. It is June twenty-third, the night our era calls St. John's Eve, but which an earlier time dedicated to the triumph of fire and the sun. In the old Europe which inherited from the Bronze Age, this great feast of the Solstice was celebrated with multitudinous small fires lit throughout the countryside. Fire and the great living sun — perhaps it would be well to honor again these two great aspects of the flame. It might help us to remember the meaning of fire before the hands and fire as a symbol. As never before, our world needs warmth in its cold, metallic heart, warmth to go on and face what has been made of human life, warmth to remain humane and kind.

XXVII

Tom Sherman and his helper, Henry Hunter, have been working at the farm. At the end of winter every house needs a carpenter as it might need a doctor, and early summer is a good time to get things done. The skylight leaked. The piazza steps had succumbed to fifteen years of snow and would have to be scrapped and replaced. There was an ominous water stain on the ceiling of the east bedroom by the outer wall, and upstairs a screen had lost its neatly-fitted runners, and mosquitoes had discovered the gap in the defense.

Every spring we have such a list, and every spring, if we can, we get hold of Tom and ask him to put us down for some "time." We do not fuss too much over the property, for any good house is as much a living and growing thing as a tomato plant or a calf, and a stability of perfection is neither wise to seek nor possible to find. So Tom puts us down as needing carpenter work, and says he will come just as soon as he has finished one or two more jobs. This understanding arrived at, we forget all about it, and go on with our usual round of things to do. We know that Tom will come when he can.

135

I didn't hear him drive up this morning, but I heard the almost simultaneous slam of two automobile doors. Looking out the kitchen window, I saw two figures walking across the grass towards the shed, one of them carrying a carpenter's box by its slot-handle. Tom had come, and on a pleasant summer day.

It was good to see him, not only because of the help he would give us, but because he is one of my oldest friends. In time of life, he stands between my generation of War I and the so-different generation of War II, a man still young, slight, wiry, and of about middle height, and dressed, that morning, in covert-cloth grey. When I first knew him, years ago, he had been working in the village shipyard which used to turn out both fishing schooners and pleasure yachts, and it was his hand which used to cut and fit the beautiful seasoned wood when the blueprint called for judgment and the craftsman's skill.

The house is full of Tom's work, and there is something else that is a part of it — a memory. Some years ago when I happened to be here alone in a forlorn spring and making a rather grim best of it, Tom — who was doing some carpentering for me — brought me a grand cake which Mrs. Sherman had been kind enough to make and send up. The thoughtful and neighborly gesture gave me just the human cheering-up I needed, for I was indeed getting rather blue.

After a morning welcome and some consulting, nobody wasted any time. The shed became a workshop, and presently sent forth the sound of sawing and hammering and an occasional discussion, the light breeze, meanwhile, blowing the curls of the shavings down the passage towards the kitchen door. The new step began to take shape, and a little later, by a certain change of sound in the use of the hammer, I guessed that Tom was working on the screens. I myself came and went to the small field and the garden patch.

At noon, Tom and Henry Hunter knocked off work and sat down and had their dinner under a tree which makes a glorious umbrella of country shade. Seeing me coming from the garden, Tom hailed me over to their side. "Do you want a swarm of bees?" he said. "I can let you have a swarm. This would be a good place to keep bees." The talk went on about bees. Henry Hunter said that his family had always had bees, and that when he was a boy the bees his father had kept were not the kind they have now "but the black bees. They used to sting like anything."

Tom told us of his adventures with wild honey, and of the old hollow hemlocks the wild swarms so often choose when they establish themselves in these vast woods. He had seen such trees raided for their store, and he remembered a giant hemlock whose hollow was a funnel of the masterless wild honey, there being such a richness and a wealth of it that "two or three wash tubs" were filled with the brown comb and the slow, dark, golden flood.

It was good talk — talk as honest, friendly, and pleasant as good bread.

FARM DIARY

Strolling groups of "cowboy" singers and "instrumentalists" are again a feature of our summer life. The troupers wear cowboy clothes of the theatrical kind with braid pipings and fancy pockets, and, to judge by their accents, come from our own New England manufacturing towns. All are rather young, and have only recently emerged from the services. The sight of one of these "cowboys" "dressed-up regardless" and walking down the street through our population of townspeople, farmers, lobstermen, clam-diggers, summer people, and craftsmen, is something for the musing observer. We go to the shows once in awhile, and always wish the youngsters well. / Sixth consecutive hot day, and we need rain badly, the farm gardens looking weighed down and frowsty with the blazing heat, and scorched spots begin to appear on the lawn. / The grass now standing high and the insect population of the fields having increased, the barn swallows are skimming the slopes, coasting the air down to the pond. / Every day, now, the children along our road go swimming in the pond, the little boys kicking up the dust and swinging their bathing trunks cheerfully as they pass; the little girls very cheerful, too, but more sedate. / Elizabeth says that a pair of redstarts are nesting somewhere near the house.

Years ago, while on a sea voyage in northern waters, I picked up a novel which some fellow passenger had abandoned under a deck chair and found myself reading it. It had to do with the efforts of two very evil men to break open the sealed and magical gate which separated the created earth and the shaped and created universe from primeval and shapeless chaos somehow lying mystically to one side. I remember a fine, last, and epic tussle between the wickedest being and the servant of man in the caves beneath a castle rooted in the sea.

There are moments in which melodrama becomes life, and this is one of them. It is not a struggle now between "good" and "bad," it is a battle between creation and chaos, between human existence and meaningless, inhuman nothingness. Perhaps there is still time to take a stand for the Kingdom of Life; it needs defenders. Perhaps, mighty as its enemies may be, allies will come who are even mightier.

XXVIII

The day is warm and the skies genial, but I have a notion that a fog bank lies just off the coast and that we shall hear from it before the long afternoon has darkened to its close. The wind which moves across this earth of fluttering and innumerable leaves is the wind which stirs when fog is near, a restless, fidgety wind which is never still in the trees, and in the sky combs out the clouds like hair. And I know the meaning of that pale and milky bank of coastal haze which lies to seaward above our country scenes of woods and fields. As soon as the earth, losing its noonday heat, grows cool with the sun descending, the fog will be upon us, taking over these blue summer skies just inland from the sea.

Even as I write, the vapor begins its slow and almost tidal advance from the horizon. The milky haze darkens and becomes a mystery of fog grey, and presently sailing fragments of the vapor are to be discovered drifting inland. The wind has not yet changed on the surface of the earth, it is still the restless southwest which is at play among the leaves and in the fruiting grass. But the southeasterly turn is coming, a breath of grey vapor, coolness, and the sea are coming towards us across the pond, coming not as a force, perhaps, but as a first physical sensation. The flying vapor is high, for the warm earth has still something to say and is lifting the wraiths into the higher air.

More arrive, and they now float between us and the earth's own cloud forms in the higher blue. Presently it is more than the vanguard which is on the move; the whole sky of the eastern horizon is following after, advancing with the vast motion of the sea across some coastal plain of sand. Yet it is not a sky which is all one mass and substance of coolness and sea-grey; it has its lower fragments, its broken vapors, and its heavy, inexorable solemnities. Already the light is changing. The east has grown grey-dark, though the earth warmth and the late afternoon sun rule tranquilly in the open west above the wall of pines.

Farmerwise, we worry about our neighbor's hay. It lies in windrows on the carpet of the shorn field, windrow upon windrow lying mounded and parallel like waves reaching the shore. The field is darkening under the darkening sky, the light upon it streaming level from the west. The neighbors, too, are apprehensive, for such an incoming of fog can mean a rainy day to follow. But help is at hand, for across our own wide field I can see the tanned figures of Carroll and his sons-in-law, Freddy and Rupert, filling the big truck: indeed, I think I see both Willa and

Elaine pitching up great forkfuls beside their men. It is done; I hear the engine start, and a first fine load is on its way to the barn.

Meanwhile, it is growing greyer and more cold. The incoming fog, moreover, is sinking as the earth chills, and I can now see a wisp of vapor between me and the pines across the road. The light grows silvery; the vapor has reached the western heavens, and is dimming and veiling over the great shield of the sun. A kind of hush seems to follow. The North Atlantic has the coast.

FARM DIARY

Hot spell ends with a turn of the wind to the N.W., and haying begins in earnest. The fine field which lies to the south of us and just beyond our line is being mowed, and the fragrance of the hay drifts towards us through the sunshine. / Fourth of July with its parades, fire crackers, and crowds over and done with. We spend the afternoon at Miss Anna Glidden's party and have a very pleasant time as always. / Wonderful visit from Ray and Hope Nash and their three youngsters, Grigg, Jon, and Holly, and a blessed evening of the best talk about the world of the human spirit. Elizabeth is Jon's godmother and I am Holly's godfather. / Many small boats on the pond, and neighbors and visitors quietly fishing in the early evening. / "Progressive" strawberries living up to their name, and yielding a good crop. / Light rain in the night, not good for the hay, but just the thing for the gardens. / Drama in the early morning: a red cow and a black cow who have strayed from their anchorage visit the farm at breakfast time. The black cow suffers herself to be recaptured easily, but the red cow, her tail flung up in a banner of rebellion, runs wildly off through the long grass of the hay slopes like a creature of the pampas. Carroll and his two sons-in-law, all quick-footed men, organize a pursuit, and finally close in upon her; she suffers her chain to be seized, and is led peaceably away.

One of the greater mischiefs which confront us today is the growing debasement of the language. Our speech is a mere shadow of its incomparable richness, having on the one hand become vulgarized and on the other corrupted with a particularly odious academic jargon. Now this is dangerous. A civilization which loses its power over its own language has lost its power over the instrument by which it thinks. Without some power over language there is neither greatness nor accuracy of thought. I am sure that this wasting disease of our English speech is one of the causes of today's bewilderment.

XXIX

We have had our first really blazing day. The sky poured down heat; the smell of hot soil rose from the cart tracks and the very fields, and wherever one looked from the farm, a blue heat-haze lay heavy on the earth. The ice truck arrived in a billow of dust and in another departed, leaving its fragmentary diamonds of chopped ice to melt to a cold dew on the grass beyond the shed. Coming to its own in the heat, our short-lived insect world made holiday, the nagging flies energized to new life and fierceness as they pestered us working in the fields.

So hot was the day that even the night was warm, and I slept with a second window open close beside my bed. Our nights, no matter what the day has been or what the set of the wind, are almost invariably cool or even autumnal cold. But this night was pleasant and warm; summer remained in our country world, brooding over field and granite ledge, over furrow holding the day's heat, and the beginning rows of northern corn.

Beyond the house and its quiet, there was only a vague world to be seen, a nocturnal world not of lines but of masses and vague shapes. Because there was no wind, not even a sigh to stir a dangling leaf, these earth masses were seemingly as without motion as a stone, the trees by the farm gate being but a solidity of darkness standing in its own dark. Yet was this world not without space. The stars were out, standing clearest overhead, and dimming as they moved low along the horizon above the other and more sombre night of earth. Nor were great Antares and the stars of the zodiacal Scorpion the only lights to be seen. It was the wonder of the night below that it had its own stars.

Over the darkness and within it moved the fireflies. The field to the south was twinkling with their lights, and to the west, between the sleeping farm and the loom of the pines, the tiny, golden-phosphorescent brilliances glowed in the dark, moving in numbers over the gloom that was the field. It was not quite a dance, this pulsation and rhythm that was at once everywhere and nowhere, nor was it on the other hand, mechanical, being so full of mystery and waywardness.

What a beautiful light it was, I thought, as I watched the glow of some one insect, pulsating on a rising flight, pass close by and against the dark of an old High-Top apple tree. It had something of moonlight to it, and something of lightning, and something of the suddenness of lightning. I am told that in certain tropical countries a field of fireflies appears to pulsate and glow in one simultaneous and inexplicable rhythm, but I have never seen such a phenomenon here, and prefer the broken and spontaneous twinkling of our own mid-summer nights. The "firefly" or "lightning bug" is a small beetle, a brownish and inoffensive creature. The light and its flashing are supposed to have something to do with the mating season. This may be so. On the other hand, the light and its flashing may simply be another example of the creative splendor and whimsicality — there is no other word — of the mystery of Nature and the earth.

FARM DIARY

Haying continues, and at the close of a blazing afternoon in a great field to the south beyond our fields, I see my friend and neighbor Carroll Winchenbaugh and his sons-in-law, Freddy French and Rupert Stevens, again pitching hay into a truck rigged as a temporary hay cart. All are stripped to the waist and brown as Indians. / Irving Oliver has planted a great field of beans. We all like our Saturday night baked beans and brown bread, and Irving's crop has a good sale. / Wild strawberries very plentiful on the hay slopes, and being patiently gathered and patiently hulled by the household. / Lawrence has arrived with the farm bell, now beautifully gilded, and has set it in its place on the cedar post by the kitchen door. / Elizabeth returns with a new summer dress very skillfully made, the pattern one of green leaves and great cheerful yellow roses on a shell-white ground.

I return to the word "whimsicality" which I used to describe one of the characteristics of Nature. Without some recognition of that element, we do not correctly weigh our visible world. In the Kingdom of Life, Nature sometimes works with a clear purpose of adaptation, constructing, for instance, those wonderful creatures, the leaf-imitating butterflies, and those living twigs, the "walking sticks." On the other side of this assumption and evidence of purpose, there exists a whole creation of pure fantasy having no explicable relation whatever between purpose and design. You see birds in the tropics that are living paint-boxes, at once exquisitely beautiful and wildly absurd. When naturalists get too serious, I like to think of this side of Nature, so creative, imaginative, and full of gusto, and of the fantastic creatures which are its jocund gift.

XXX

"I have here a small pitcher with blue and yellow flowers. How much am I offered? Fifty. Who'll make it seventy-five? Seventy-five, who'll make it a dollar? A dollar: who'll make it a dollar and a quarter? A dollar and a quarter I have: who'll make it a dollar-fifty? Anybody make it a dollar-fifty? Any bids? Sold to the lady in the brown hat for a dollar and a quarter."

It is the very perfection of a summer's day, and on a side street of the seacoast town and on the lawn of an old white house, a whole miscellany of household goods stands in the open air under two venerable elms. There are old benches covered with kitchen china and table china, a parlor organ, chairs of all kinds, some arranged in rows, boxes of old books, pictures stacked dustily, their backs to the observer, wooden bowls and egg beaters, and spool beds and horsehide trunks.

Auctions are a part of our adventure of the summer. We all go to them when they are held nearby, especially if we knew the family whose things are being auctioned off. We buy agricultural tools and implements at farm auctions, and at town auctions are liable to bid for what takes our fancy. Because we are an old, a conservative, and a thrifty people, and shipbuilders and sea-farers withal, there is no telling here what an auction may bring to light. I have seen a small cottage on the coast produce a superbly carved ceremonial comb from the old Bight of Benin, and as for grandfathers' clocks, they used to take them home in hayracks, carefully laid flat on a cushion of new hay.

The weather being so fine, and the auction so well advertised, a sizable number of townspeople and summer people have gathered in the driveway and on the lawn. There is also a figure I have never known to be absent from any auction anywhere — somebody's black and tan hound-dog seated not on his sitdown, but on the small of his back and trying perseveringly to scratch the bottom of his chin.

People are coming, people are going, small boys are moving about, the usual antique dealers are turning plates over, and buyers are carrying various purchases off to their parked cars. Going about in the throng, our summer people enliven the entire scene with modern color and gaiety. "How much am I offered?" "No, Mam, I wouldn't say it was an antique." "Don't know what you'd call this —" Pause, and an answer from many ladies replying antiphonally, "It's a tea-tray." A spirited battle takes place over a "Boston rocker" painted black and gold with an oriental bird in golden scrollwork on the headboard.

In terms of town and village history, I know well what I am seeing. It is not only the last of some old household which is being scattered to the wolves, but the lares and penates of America's early nineteenth century. This "omnium gatherum" of furniture is our 1840's and 1850's with the usual few — and bad — additions from the 1870's plus something of the flowery-bowery world of the bouncing early 1900's. Browsing among the pictures, I find that old-time favorite, "A Yard of Kittens," and behind it a particularly good late eighteenth-century portrait-engraving of President George Washington seated in his Presidential chair.

"I think you'll like what he's putting up now," says Elizabeth quickly. "Let's go closer."

"I now show you," begins the auctioneer, and not only do I like what he holds up to view but I feel that it would take a charge of bears to separate me from it. It is a painting, a "genuine oil painting," about twenty inches square and framed in a gay but not too gaudy gilt frame of the late eighties or the nineties.

Now pictures are my weakness, and this is a prize. Done by some rustic and inspired amateur about fifty or sixty years ago, it depicts in fine, bold color a scene full of dramatic action and bravura, the departure of a horsedrawn fire engine from the engine house. The back of the picture is the engine house archway full of golden light, and the foreground is the engine itself pouring out a long tress of wonderful smoke

150

while two gigantic dapple-grey horses plunge forward in an artistic moment of outstretched necks and lashing hoofs. They are neither real horses nor rocking horses, but a combination of the two such as only a genius could achieve. A fireman in blue with handlebar moustaches leans forward to drive, and a second figure leans out from the fire box.

"Sold to Mr. Beston for three dollars and fifty cents!"

We have hung it in the winter kitchen beside the fireplace, and the horses have been promptly christened "Major" and "Prince."

FARM DIARY

The early summer festival of bird song is now a thing of the past, and though we hear birds during the day, it is usually only a casual cheeping and twittering that we catch. Every once in a while, of course, we are still favored with an unexpected song. / Buyers from the lumber companies are visiting the farm country, purchasing what timber they can locate, and farmers who have scrub timber on the backroads have many of them made a deal. / Haying season in full swing, leaving dangling wisps of hay on the bushes beside the farm roads, and fields of dry, golden stubble which a first rain will color through with green. / Squash bugs under control, but some of these modern chemical replacements and strengthenings of the still scarce Rotenone can do things to one's hide when they mix in with sweat. / Good swimming in the pond, a wonderful treat at the end of a hot day. / Just at twilight, on an evening of sea fog and wailing wind, discover a large porcupine in a poplar sapling, swaying to and fro in the chill, melancholy gusts. / Elizabeth says that a kind of bright pine-green seems to be the favorite color of the new cars on Route 1.

The other day, while looking at an album of good modern photographs of ancient Greek portrayals of the old classical life, many of them entirely "realistic," I found myself wondering what the quality was in these ancient faces which is absent from ours. The modern face is a tired one, but it was not the absence of fatigue which interested me in these countenances of the past. They too must have known their times of weariness. What was it? Assurance? Acceptance? A sense of roots in an objective world?

I give no answer to my own question. Of one thing, however, I am sure: these people did not ask too much. Perhaps asking too much is an error more dangerous than we realize, a thing of strong poison to the human soul. Our world would do well for awhile to muse upon the serenity and happiness possible within our human and earthly limitations.

XXXI

It is summer, the season of leaves and grass and the everchanging fancies of the flowing winds, and all day long there seem a thousand things to do. Weeds and pests are now to be fought, and the hay mows filled against the winter: the bright sunshine and the warmth must be made every use of while they last. The scissor-clatter sound of mowing machines begins the working day; and the afternoon sun beats down on bare backs, the steely gleam of hay fork tines, and the lifted bundles of hay falling into the old hayracks swaying and rolling over these hillside fields. Thirsty afternoons, and worthy of the pause by the deep well or the battered enamel cup standing by the spring.

Not owning a mowing machine, I do what so many do here and make a "dicker" with a neighbor to come and cut the hay. The neighbor who comes and helps us is Randall Simmons, and when he arrives in the morning after the sun has dried the fields, he brings his whole family with him for the haying. An old truck drives in and while two small shirtless boys are clambering out from somewhere, Randall and his wife Frances and a pair of tiny little girls are scrambling out from the driver's seat. As I walk towards the family, I see Randall stop a moment and look with a studying eye at the uncut grass and the silvery morning clouds beginning to drift along the edges of the sky.

Randall is about thirty. He is shirtless, too, lean in body but rugged and muscular, and outdoor work and sun have tanned him to an Indian brown. Frances is slim and blonde and tall, and often wears old shorts for her work in the field. The costume sounds sophisticated, but so thoroughly is Frances a young farm wife that she might be a girl from some Scythian or Spartan farm.

The children are all of them as flaxen-haired as children in an old-fashioned German Christmas card. The boys are Ordway and Ernest, the girls Rowena and Cherry, and Ordway, who is the oldest, is between nine and ten.

I find it touching to watch the family work together. While Ordway and his father are busy together in one region of the fields, Frances and Ernest will be somewhere else running an improvised tractor and the wheeled rake. Ernest is but a little boy — I doubt if he is yet seven — yet the rake is his chore and task, and on its seat he rides obeying a sign from his mother to lift the curved iron teeth when she has built a windrow into proper line. The two little girls have their chance when the hay is being lifted to the truck. Like tiny maenads in rumpled dresses, they dance up and down on the load, treading down the grass

154

while the late afternoon sun turns their tangled flaxen locks into silken aureoles.

It is done, the truck has a first load, and away they go, the two boys riding the load, the girls on the seat with their mother. I look across my shorn fields and am glad to see the clean stubble stretching from the farm lawn to the stone wall and the darkness of the pines. Randall has left his new and bright red mowing machine under the shelter of a paternal oak; the rake stands deserted in the open field. The farm still lives and carries on its pattern of being. Shadows are lengthening, and the sun silvering, and in a little while I shall hear from the pines that music like a melody of tiny bells which is the song of the hermit thrush.

FARM DIARY

Bolt of lightning strikes a friend's house; does no particular damage to the dwelling, but kills every minnow in a pail of bait left in the cool of the cellar. / More auctions enliven the neighborhood, and at one such gathering Elizabeth bids in a Turkey-red kitchen tablecloth in excellent condition. Very cheerful for winter use. / The small dog, happy in the summer weather, has taken to snoozing in the full sunlight of the south doorway. / Every saltwater creek and inlet now to have its great blue heron, and every pond shore its solitary sandpiper. /

Strawberry season over; no more shortcakes at supper. Now come blueberry muffins. / Irving Oliver reports the huge muddy hoof prints of a moose in the woods beyond the clearing made by a portable saw mill. / The spring having been so cold and late, all of us are hoping for a mild and lingering fall. My tomatoes continue to thrive. / Under a half moon in the summer twilight, village boys fishing a backwater of the pond for the huge horn pout or "bullheads" of those waters. These fish make an excellent chowder and are good fried.

One of the complications of the problem of the machine is the fact that just as certain people are born hunters and farmers, others are born machinists. The mechanical strain is in humanity, and if it has given us a machine civilization increasingly difficult to manage, it has also given us the wheel and the knife. I do not forget that memorable saying of my old friend Edward Gilchrist that "the secret of the artificer is the secret of civilization." Yet what we must ask today is whether or not the mechanist strain has increased out of all bounds, and taken over an undue proportion of the way of life. It is well to use the wheel but it is fatal to be bound to it.

XXXII

The week began with two hot and "muggy" days. So lifeless was the hazy air that there was scarce enough higher wind to float the woolpack clouds through the dulled heavens, and such a breeze as moved low upon the earth stirred no curtains at the open windows of the farm. A third day began with grey cloud and the same passive air lying almost stagnant upon the heated land, but at noon came a change of the wind, a darkening overhead, and the first small, scattering drops of rain.

Oh blessedness and wonder of the rain! Not for weeks had we seen such drops, and with their appearance the long tension of a dry spell broke like a thin globe of imaginary glass. Calling and replying to each other across the rain-pitted water, loons began their quaverings and trills: they always have something to say when rain begins. Then to the senses came that first country smell of dust and rain, and then a smell of wet earth and rain, and this was presently followed by a cool breath of air moving with the rain along the fields and fragrant with a faint, cool smell of grass. A moment later a neighbor's cat slunk past me in the garden, and took shelter under the barn.

Our gardens which had been standing still from dryness would now awake. The earth was drinking in the showers. In the small vegetable patch, the rain sluiced over the top leaves of the bush squashes, and trickled and fell from their surfaces down into the lesser leaves and the coarse, handsome, yellow-orange blossoms, and off by themselves, the strawberry plants, lovers of water, put on a varnished glisten of rain and cleanliness. In another field, rain-soaked and seen through rain, the corn stood refreshed and seemingly turned to a bluer green than it appears under daylight and the sun.

In the next field south, a neighbor walked down to unfasten a staked-out cow, and followed her at a peaceful saunter to his barn. Looking about the landscape, I saw that everywhere in sight the open earth of the planted ground had changed color: it had been sunbaked and pale, it was now a light brown darkening with every drop. The long rows of beans would be all the greener by tomorrow morning. They had needed just this.

The rain was not heavy but the earth was getting a good drenching. Standing near an ancient apple tree, I could hear the whispering rain sound in its leaves and the muffled hum and beat of the rain sound from the earth everywhere about, and hearing rejoiced in the renewal of the mysterious bond between the clouds and all that has life below.

It was still raining when I went about in the

quiet, and put the house to bed. Standing at the screen of the front door, I could hear the deep living sound in the darkness beyond, sound of earth and rain, sound of promise and life.

FARM DIARY

In a mowed field at New Harbor, a group of men are spreading out the great fishing nets. The careful work, the slow, considered gestures, the checked shirts, the old village, and the ocean beyond its trees and roofs — all blend together to make a salty memory. / Talking with Lester Dunbar, he tells me that in the past many farms planted a piece of barley and had barley bread on the table. / The farm hay now cut to the last usable plume of red top and timothy, and the last great load of hay drives up the shorn slopes to the level land by the house. / Dogday weather, and the water in the pond as still as water in a rain barrel. Today a motionless boat with two pensive fishermen floats in the placid scene. / Farm kitchen a busy place these hot days with the neighbors who have been doing the mowing coming in for a drink of spring water, and four little, thirsty, flaxen-haired country children wanting a drink too./ Elizabeth answers the new telephone and returns to tell me that we have a second Damariscotta grandnephew, Daniel Thomas Day, and that he weighed nine pounds.

This is not a wheat country though we can grow it here; our fields are fields of corn. Beautiful as such a field may be when the corn is standing high and the great harsh leaves stir with their grating sound in the hot August wind, it is often of the wheat that I think, of the ancient plant which is the token and symbol of man and of order and civilization, of the wheat of Egypt and the threshing floors, of the bright mornings of the harvest and the golden, burning afternoons, and of the last sheaf brought home in rustic triumph from the fields.

We have a tradition which is carried on by thoughts and words: has it been remarked that tradition is also carried on by things? Wheat itself is tradition, and good bread is tradition; not without reason have the great religions honored the breaking of bread together. Perhaps it would be well for us to recognize this body of tradition which lies in things and be more aware of it. We have grown blind to it and forget that apart from words it binds human being to human being, and that a way of life must seek to preserve the strengths whose roots go deep.

XXXIII

It was the hilltop field with the mowed hay lying in windrows in the heat. To the north and down the hill, beyond a pasture and a narrow wood, lay the pond and its blue distances; to the south stood a stone wall, and over it, in a summer blaze of light, the immense and fiery sun. I was just in time for the beginning of the afternoon's work. From close beside the barn, a very modern tractor painted green and yellow had set out on its journey to the fields, dragging behind it an ancestral hayrack once painted carriage blue.

Every year when the mowing machines begin their clatter in the fields, and the tall grass falls flat beside them in long and even rows, I look forward to working with my neighbor Hudson Vannah at his farm across the pond. We are old friends, and during the war years I pitched hay with him on many a long, hot summer afternoon with the war planes now and then passing over-head. Help was scarce then; it is none too plenti-ful now.

It took me but a moment to reach for my hay fork in the back of the car, and step across the stone wall into the field. So dry has been our early summer that the stubble underfoot had

161

burnt to gold, and round and about the stubble roots the earth itself lay dry. On came the tractor and the rack, the old wagon rolling about as in a seaway over the unevenness of the hot and golden earth, with the haymakers clinging to its side.

A twelve-year-old boy in shoes and overall pants and nothing more was driving the tractor and managing it and its course with sureness and skill. All the authority of manhood was in his face, I thought, as I saw his boy's hand reach for the great lever at his side. This was Ronnie Winslow, a neighbor's son.

Earle Baldwin was there from the farm just across from us, a fine lad who was honor man at our academy, and came back from the Army with a sergeant's stripes. And Dale was with us, a veteran of World War I who is here in summer, and Hudson himself, who followed behind with the great hand hayrake.

Still in his thirties, spare, well-knit, muscular, and tireless, perhaps a trifle under middle height, Hudson never seems to rest, and many is the time I have gone past his farm in the twilight and seen him working busily and all alone in his thriving and never-neglected fields. He has a herd of milking shorthorns, and there is a tin sign saying so swinging at his gate.

There is no work on a farm I like better than work in the hayfields on a blazing day. Puff, puff, puff — and the green and yellow tractor hauled the rack beside a windrow, and plunge went each fork into the sun-hot, the almost crisp-dry hay. On this part of the field a stand of timothy had grown strong and high, and lifting up a forkful of hay, one had to tear it from its intricate entanglement with other stalks — drag at it till it gave and could be lifted up to the rack. In other places where there was a touch of water in the ground, I found myself tossing up a different type of grass like so much fluff.

Oh, work that is done in freedom out of doors, work that is done with the body's and soul's goodwill, work that is an integral part of life and is done with friends — is there anything so good? The youngster had jumped down from the tractor and climbed onto the rack to tread down the rising hill of hay. Our forks clicked as they met together and he speared down my load; sweat ran into my eyes and chaff glued itself to my skin; higher and higher, fork by fork, up-tumbled and rose the load with the urchin surefooted and busy in the fragrant sea.

As we were bringing the last load, something very lovely came to pass. A great eagle rose from somewhere on the top of the hill, planed above us, began the vast circles of his climbing, and disappeared into the evening and the blue.

FARM DIARY

Towards the twentieth of July we begin to

163

say goodby to the bobolinks. First they stop singing, and then they go, melting out of the landscape all at once like a "dissolving view" in an old-fashioned stereopticon lecture in the town hall. / More and more the town next door takes on the summer look, and becomes a bewilderment of out-of-state cars, crowded stores, trailers parked on side streets, and visitors in gaudy and carefree summer clothes; with every "ye olde" something or other on Route 1 doing a rushing business. Gave road directions the other day to a big car with a British license and a British righthand drive. / Striped "cucumber beetles" a real nuisance this year; have to keep spraying and dusting all the time. There are times when I think some pests regard arsenate of lead as an exhilarating marmalade. / Even the trees are showing the effect of the dry weather, the birches yellowing and the sumacs turning an autumn red. / Elizabeth has bought from a neighbor a pair of blankets made from the wool of his sheep. Some small mill in the boundary mountains makes them up for him. Color a good blue, and the texture well-woven, light and warm. I thought them a bit expensive, but he sells every pair, and they are certainly good, honest workmanship and good material.

Has it occurred to any one that as civilization

has become more urbanized and city populations greater than those who live by agriculture, there has been a parallel increase in war and violence? Apparently some relation exists which is not entirely economic. The farmer would reply that agriculture is an art of peace which requires a peaceful time, and that agricultural populations, as seen in history, are not by nature aggressively military. A population of planters and farmers, moreover, can not leave its crops to shift for themselves and gather themselves together into barns. The machine, on the contrary, can be left to shift for itself. It does not improve it, but it can be deserted on its concrete floor. Above all, the machine world is barren of that sense of responsibility which is the distinguishing spiritual mark and heritage of the long ownership of land. I think history would agree that though spears may be beaten into pruning hooks, pruning hooks are less frequently beaten into spears.

XXXIV

It is late at night on Federal Route 1, the Atlantic Highway of the maps. The traffic is no such traffic as one may find at the entrance of any city; nevertheless, on it goes, relentless though not continuous, the trucks coming out of some tunnel of pines glowing with starry lights like rushing constellations. The farm lies about three miles from the route, and in summer when the nights are still and the wind is due south, I can sometimes hear the far, far away sound of some wheeled monster changing gears on our long climb to the eastward. What are they carrying? Barrels and crates of food, probably, those going east and north carrying in more food for our augmented population, those going south and west carrying the local catch of sea food to the cities up the coast.

But I intend to devote no chronicle to Route 1. For the greater part of its length, as it crosses the state, it is a vulgar confusion of predatory billboards and trashy signs which are destructively allowed to steal and exploit one of the great landscapes of the nation. I take courage in the fact that the village has not thus sold its birthright and its soul, and that as you cross it and its fields, you will have great views of the forest and the coastal mountains. What interests me about Route 1 is its place in the village economy. Our season is short, our northern winters glorious and cold, and for many a household on Route 1, the highway helps earn the family living.

The cars pass, cars from all over the Union, cars from Massachusetts and from California and Idaho, and many trailers, I notice, from the mountain West. As the stream passes, our various farms on the highway begin rather modestly to display their wares. A small board painted white and lettered in black or dark blue serves as a tug at the sleeve as you go by.

We manage to offer, I think, quite a variety of things. Our salesroom may be the kitchen with its morning fire dying out, or the front parlor with its cottage organ and the family Bible; a pocket-sized booth or the open lawn. We have country hooked rugs and braided rugs — these we hang on a clothesline near the road and in the shade. We have pieced quilts, we have toys and toy lobster pots, we have miniature sea gulls, we have antiques — they can be anything these days — we have doughnuts in a crock and excellent home-made bread and fresh jams properly made with this summer's plenty of sugar. At Ralph and Doris Keene's, an old-fashioned curlicue "what-not" stands by the hollyhocks and the side door, genially garnished with summer vegetables. And the cars whiz on or stop, and we make change out of an old cigar box with a lid.

No local sign is more characteristic than a

167

board saying "Kittens." We are great cat-traders, our cats being the famous "Maine shags" of the old coast. These cats of ours, often thought to be some out-of-the-way variety of Persian, are not Persians at all but the hardy, long-haired cat of northern Manchuria, and the race is said to have been introduced here by some trading sea captain in the early nineteenth century. They are good cats and have personality. Purchasers usually have to knock at the kitchen door and wait till the balls of fluff are coaxed from under the stove. Such kittens, moreover, are often shipped instead of being given over directly to the automobilists.

And so it goes; the little trading venture being now at its height. It is good for us, for it not only adds a new interest to the summer but it gives us a wider idea of the great nation behind us to the west. When winter comes, we shall talk of the pleasant visit from the people with the Wisconsin number-plates, and the lady from New Jersey who bought the home-made bread every Tuesday morning. I've never kept store myself, not being on the Route, but I think I shall have to get some friend to let me try it for a day.

FARM DIARY

As we return from the evening movies, the headlight glare picks up a fox cub sitting in the middle of the country road. He runs ahead of us awhile, and then runs off to one side into the grass of a field. He seems more yellow in color than red, which makes us mistake him at a distance for a barn cat. / Autumn tent-caterpillars spinning their destructive webs on various old apple trees. / While talking with a charming lady about the living relation here of the sea and the old coastal towns, she tells me that in her girlhood she was on a ship wrecked by a typhoon off the coast of Formosa. / We share the last hot-spell with the rest of the world, and when it ends, we do not have summer again, but a clear cool foretaste of September. / Fishing communities now holding their "Fisherman's Festivals" with shore dinners and "all the lobster you can eat for a dollar." What I like to see is the show of the fisherman's handicrafts and the actual weaving of nets and lobster pot heads. A show put on, I suppose, for our summer visitors, and one which is both interesting and humanly right.

When this twentieth century of ours became obsessed with a passion for mere size, what was lost sight of was the ancient wisdom that the emotions have their own standards of judgment and their own sense of scale. In the emotional world a small thing can touch the heart and the imagination every bit as much as something impressively gigantic; a fine phrase is as good as an epic, and a small brook in the quiet of a wood can have its say with a voice more profound than the thunder of any cataract.

Who would live happily in the country must be wisely prepared to take great pleasure in little things. Country living is a pageant of Nature and the year; it can no more stay fixed than a movement in music, and as the seasons pass, they enrich life far more with little things than with great, with remembered moments rather than the slower hours. A gold and scarlet leaf floating solitary on the clear, black water of the morning rain barrel can catch the emotion of a whole season, and chimney smoke blowing across the winter moon can be a symbol of all that is mysterious in human life.

XXXV

The side road leaves Route 1 at the top of a wooded hill. For a few level miles it leads on through a ragged farming country, then climbing a steep knoll, presently opens on a great and widening view of mountains, a blue pond, and an agricultural landscape set about with thriving farms. At one end of the pond is a pleasant, old-fashioned village in its elms, and about a mile beyond, its location marked by rows of parked autos massed in a trodden field, is the Fair. It is only a small fair but it is our fair, and already the distant squeal of mechanical music floats to us across the green meadows and the rural scene.

The farm family has long had a warm place in its heart for the fair at Union Village. Our smaller fairs have been one of the casualties of the war, either ceasing to be or dragging on a poor existence as horse races tied to shabby carnivals, but the Union Fair has kept its popularity and retained its standing as a genuine old-style agricultural show. It has its horses and its cattle, its great yokes of oxen and its bulls with nose rings and blue ribbons, its handicrafts and quilts and jars of vegetables, its horse races and its contests, its gypsy fortune tellers, and its giant swings.

171

Well, let's go in. "This way, please. Easy now. OK." A pleasant, well-mannered Boy Scout with various Scout badges and a very grown up and professional police badge, shows us where to park; the doors slam, and away to the fair we go.

Almost at once there is something fine to see. The great teams of farm horses which are going to enter the dragging contests are coming down the field from their quarters with each owner standing on the stoneboat dragged behind, and holding the reins with the look and assurance of a Roman charioteer in overalls. The brass harness studs and buckles shine like brazen gold in the beautiful morning light; gaudy plumes bob on the huge heads, and the brushed tails have the grace of waterfalls. A fine pair of strawberry roans take my eye as down the slope they go to the little grandstand and the dragging area.

"Hello, George. Showing here?" "Yes, got a first prize yesterday for the Guernsey bull." "Hello, Randall, I suppose you've brought your steers?" "Yes, going in this afternoon. The kid here got second yesterday with his yoke." Yellow-haired Ordway, aged nine, grins shyly. "Ordway, you show Mr. and Mrs. Beston your red ribbon."

The oxen are all of them in their shed. There are many yokes, for the country round Union is one of the last regions of the republic to rear and use these great Virgilian beasts. They handle better than horses when our winter comes with its deeps and drifts of snow. Going to the dragging contests for oxen, we see the real thing in drivers, a country boy about fifteen years old who looks as if he came from some small farm. When his steers pull, he throws, as it were, his will in with theirs, and placing his hand on the flank of the nigh ox, drives forward not only with his urging voice and his eagerness but also with his leaning body — the boy and his great creatures all in one rhythm of work and rustic ambition.

It is interesting to watch, and I am glad when he carries off a prize.

Such a medley of impressions force themselves all at once on the senses that it is hard not to be a bit confused when strolling about in the heart of the fair. The smell of popcorn and the din of loudspeakers. Other smells of coffee urns and frying hamburgers. The rustic smell of farm animals, and the smell of trodden grass and earth.

On the midway, I see some gypsy women with beaded purses at their hips, standing by the entrances to their fortune-telling booths. I always wish them a polite "good-day" in Romany, a friend once having taught me certain greeting words. The stunt at first silences them with an immense suspicion, and then they all laugh merrily and wickedly, and give Elizabeth and me special recognition when we pass. We have one gypsy word well established in the English language — our word "pal," which is the gypsy for comrade.

So sauntering about, we reach our car, and drive off full of plans for the next fair.

Our friend and neighbor John Buchan comes with his trowels and mortar, and repairs the back of the great fireplace, neatly setting in new bricks. Three chimneys get cleaned in the afternoon, the dust and crumbs of acccumulated soot filling pail after pail, and, last job of the day, John checks all five chimneys at the roof. / Summer camps closing up everywhere, and great truck-loads of camp trunks and heavy suitcases are rolling down our country roads to the small town railroad stations. / Another bear reported seen on one of the nearby saltwater peninsulas. / Blue jays are leaving the pasture woodlots and coming down towards the farmhouses; I counted five this morning stirring about in our biggest apple tree, and we hear an unusual variety of calls. / What a good dish a "summer cabbage" makes when properly cooked and properly buttered and flavored! / Lawrence back with us for a day's work, bringing with him not only his shock of sunburnt yellow hair and his cheerful self, but also a great two-handled basket of his own vegetables as a present for the farm.

Every once in a while, when one lives in the

country and observes wild animals, one is sure to come upon dramas and acts of courage which profoundly stir the heart. The tiniest birds fight off the marauder, the mother squirrel returns to the tree already scorched by the on-coming fire; even the creatures in the pond face in their own strange fashion the odds and the dark. Surely courage is one of the foundations on which all life rests! I find it moving to reflect that to man has been given the power to show courage in so many worlds, and to honor it in the mind, the spirit, and the flesh.

XXXVI

Every time I go shopping to Damariscotta, and especially on Saturday afternoons, I meet the fishermen on the street or in the stores, bronzed and sunburnt as the sea does the weathering, and marked by the folded-over rubber boots which are the sign of the craft. I come upon them now buying groceries, now buying marine hardware and coils of new line, now reading the morning paper and waiting their turn in the barber's chair. Because it is cool, even cold at sea, they wear their flannel shirts and woolen pants through the year, sewing bold patches everywhere when the old cloth wears through.

I call them fishermen, but the term and the rubber boots loosely includes the run of our people who live by the sea. There are true fishermen among them with their own boats, there are clammers whom the state authorities are forever checking; there are lobstermen with their boats and lobster traps, there are diggers of the seaworms which are used for bait; this last is now among us a very profitable trade. Whatever they may chance to be, and whether boat owners or clammers, one great influence binds them all together; they are people of the sea. Fiercely independent, courageous, and, according to some, jestingly truculent when in the mood, they drive to town in their old cars from their coves and villages, and will have nothing but the best when they buy.

Herring from the weirs are now selling for over $15 a barrel at the wharf, and lobsters are high and the late summer catch a good one, but it is not prices which hold these neighbors to their craft. Not for them are the hay fork, the plough, and the barn shovel, but the bait tub, the salt box, and the barbed hook; not for such as these the rooted fields but the more perilous and unquiet pastures of the blue. Before the automobile opened up the coast the fishing villages were isolated and apart, a situation reflected in the character of the towns. The last fisherman to wear an ear plug of gold — an inheritance from Elizabethan England — was an oldtimer at Monhegan Island, and it is not so very long ago since he gave up forever his sheath knife and the sea.

Your true fishermen with their own boats and gear are the natural leaders and nobility of the craft. Today most of them are young or youngish men, for the old fisherman — as a figure — largely vanished with the great days of sail. Nowadays, moreover, a man with a boat has to be a competent engineer; his life depends upon it. Many of our sea folk, too, are light haired, and this I take to be a reflection of the Scandinavian blood in the British strain which first colonized these coves and isles.

Because I am living on fresh water and on a farm, these are not my people, though I stretch out a hand to them for I am seacoast born and bred. But I know something of the life which they carry on in our cold and brilliant waters with the great mountain-shaped hills rising blue against the lonely inland sky. I know the lonely coves in the spruce-clad coast line, and the rocks over which the rising tide breaks in a crystalline smother of tumbling and rolling foam. And the bitter seas of winter, too, are theirs with the driving vapors of icy days drifting low above the waves and hiding the foundation of the islands behind their scarves of mist.

A hardy folk. If our doctrinaires have put upon men's shoulders more than they can or are willing to carry, and we pass into some slavery to a cannibal form of the state, these sea folk will be the last to wear the tattooed mark. It will not be easy to overcome the heritage of the other disciplines and freedoms of the sea. So I like to see the sheath knives and the rubber boots and the patches and the direct eyes. They are something to hold on to in any nation.

FARM DIARY

Over the open regions of the local countryside fly small lemon-yellow butterflies. Now they go their way alone, now two are maneuvering together, now three or four seem to

178

have some sort of temporary association. Meanwhile, the earth of the hay fields is alive with frisky grasshoppers. / Returning across the pond at twilight, I send the canoe close along the wooded shoreline, and think to myself that though the day here belongs to the white man, the night is still the Indian's. / Elizabeth gone to Massachusetts on a short visit, and I become a hermit living with a small dog in a very empty house. / Sweet corn still coming in from the gardens, and only yesterday our neighbor Louise Winchenbaugh sends us over a batch of unusually tender and delicious Golden Bantam. / Our population of swallows has deserted us, flying south to the sea, then south and westward along the marshes of the coast.

As I watch the fire burning in the great fireplace on a first chilly night, I do not wonder that fire and the mystery of fire have played so important a part in the great religions of mankind. The power to kindle that ever-hungry flame must have been the first great achievement of man on his way to fuller being; with fire he both metaphorically and in all reality could see ahead in to the dark. "Fire is a good servant but a bad master." So runs the proverb. I can remember hearing it said in the long ago. To me, it is the element which is always a part of the mystery and beauty of the world. The earth may be shabbily and wickedly broken, the river and the air befouled, but the living flame, rising from whatever source, is beauty from its first appearance and as beauty lives. There is no compromise with flame, and not without reason has it served us as a symbol of that unknown to whose ultimate mystery we can but lift our uncertain hands.

XXXVII

The other day, while visiting with friends, I chanced to follow a path which led to a river across a kind of blueberry pasture heavily over-grown with goldenrod. The hour was close to noon, the day sunny and very still, and from all about me and the earth world at my feet I could hear the myriad and continuous hum of insects working in the bright expanse of yellow flowers. Finding the place and the sound of interest, I stood for a little time at a turn of the path, inclosed, as it were, in some great hollow shell filled with the insect music of the earth. I took it as a kind of farewell of that strange and alien world of insect life which lives beside our own and disputes our human overlordship. These cold nights of early September are the twilight of the insect mystery; in a little while our rivals will be gone, and the north again belong to us and the snow.

Every year at the farm I watch the insect kingdom come into its northern being, flourish in what we have of heat and sun, live out its myriad life, and disappear almost as if it had never been. Though on warm days in mid-winter one may sometimes see in the woods some solitary and out-of-season "fly" only an entomologist could name, our insect world is essentially a presence and a manifestation of heat and light which rises to its very ecstasy of insect being on days when the sun glares unbearably, the earth cakes, and the garden flowers droop their wilted leaves.

Heat it is which rules and maddens that curious world. It is when the sun burns above that the deer-fly plagues us in the fields, circling furiously about our heads and striking at us with its darting, poisonous bite, it is then that the great dragonflies hunt the borders and the waters of the pond, then that the moths come of nights to knock clumsily against the screens of lighted rooms, and flutter aimlessly and foolishly over the incomprehensible mesh of wire. We are aware of the world most responsively, perhaps, when it annoys us and we have to wage battle with its swarming appetites, yet harmless butterflies can please us like children with their frivolity and beauty, and we can stare at some small crawling monster and begin thinking of Nature's unappreciated and too-little considered adventures in the world of the grotesque.

An alien, an ever alien world, and to be honest, one that sometimes chills the blood as do those magnified photographs which show the insect mask — for they are a faceless tribe — the insect mask with its dragon jaws and stony, expressionless, ten thousand similar eyes. Moralists tell us to go to the ant and be wise, but the ant has always seemed to me a dull creature without joy and a tremendous nuisance in the pantry. Of all the kingdom man has been able to place but one creature under the shadow of his hand — the honey bee — that fierce, small thing from which he has nothing he does not obtain by guile.

Where should we be, we shall have to ask, without the aid of this kingdom in pollination? We should be in a sorry case indeed, our orchards and gardens reduced to skeletons and ghosts of what they should be in quality, yield, and vitality of seed. Nature has many a trick with pollens, calling to the aid of her passion for life all kinds of curious floral mechanisms for self-pollination and the powers of the wind. Self-pollination, however, has two sides, now being a casual business, now a final and desperate trick when all else has failed. When our orchards bear, let us be grateful to the bees, and remember that man has a number of food plants which some special insect alone can pollinate.

I write these lines late at night in the big kitchen, alone at the table by "the dead and drowsy fire." But a moment ago, I saw a small darkish something move upon the linoleum square which fills the center of the floor: it was a field cricket, the first invader of the year. We shall have many such refugees when the nights grow even more cold, and an autumnal moon rides high above the leafless trees and grass that will be frosty in the morning. I had forgotten that the cricket, too, was a part of our human life and its tradition. He shall hide tonight where he will.

West and south along Route 1, the visiting cars whiz by us with their out-of-state number plates, homeward bound through the bright September days. / School begins, and on a country road near an old, one-room schoolhouse of mellowed brick, a boy of nine or ten is carrying a fresh pail of drinking water back for the "scholars." We use the old word here. / Myrtle warblers moving south and taking their time about it pause at the farm, and sample the red berries of the Tartarian honeysuckle. / In the pleasant bouquets which Elizabeth puts in the parlor I notice for the first time a tiny branch of autumn leaves included with the yellow autumn flowers.

I understand from various friends that there is a campaign going on in rural areas to re-open our old-fashioned, one-room country schools. Well . . . one might go farther and fare worse. What such schools used to be able to give us is something we very badly need, and that is a real first sense of being a member of a definite community. Without more of that sense than we now have, there is not much sensible hope of the better nation out of which must come the better world. The big, over-crowded modern schools with their parades and drum-majorettes and courses in "citizenship" just do not give this vital sense of human association. I shall watch any such small school experiment with interest, and so here's a Porter apple for dear teacher, and may the children be sent home early when the afternoon darkens and the stove glows red, and the snow begins to fall.

XXXVIII

From the hilltop of the farm I now look forth on a landscape divided as a map might be into three colors, each with its domain. Within the girdle of our northern pines I see the blue of the September pond, the brown of uncut grassland, and everywhere the beautiful new green which has carpeted the fields whose hay was cut in summer when the sun was high. A mood and a quiet of autumn brood upon the land, and maples thrust out flaming branches from trees which have something of an end-of-summer air.

So cloudless and so glowing are the days, so warm and still the bright autumnal hours that we tend to forget what the sky to the northwest has stored away for us of bitter cold and "the treasures of the snow." It is the night which brings the warning and the winter bell, the night ever more swiftly at hand, the night which with every hour rolls up its own pageant of winter from the east. One comes gratefully back to the kitchen from our autumnal nights, and throws a fresh billet on the fire.

Last night, soon after supper, I had to go down the road to see a neighbor, and when I returned to the farm, the full moon was rising through a dark which promised frost. Before the rising of the disk, a pool of light gathered above on a low, thin cloud, and glowingly brightened until the satellite itself appeared and rose above the woods. As the full orb cleared the earth I could see outlined upon its face, as if arranged there by some old-fashioned, romantic artist, the silhouetted height of a great ragged pine which crowns the ridge. It seemed to me as I stood there that some vibration or wave of night and life accompanied the overflowing and revelation of the moon, for I soon heard an owl cry in my woods and far away a dog barked from a farm on the other side.

Because I have always had a kind of piety for the beauty and the mystery of the night, finding in that great starlit splendor a peace which day does not harbor and cannot give, I lingered outdoors and watched awhile. There would be a frost; it was growing bitterly cold. Presently I became aware of something very curious and beautiful to see. The surface of the pond being warmer than the frosty air which had so swiftly succeeded the pleasant warmth of the day, the moonlit waters were beginning to mist over and breathe forth moonlit wreaths and veils of vapor like a cauldron of ghosts such as an Indian hunter might tell about when he resumed to his own people from the woods.

Burnished by the moon, its levels veiled with the vapor as it arose, the pond looked as motionless and cold as I have ever chanced to see it. It was not the pond in winter: it was the pond at some mysterious ending of an age in time. Higher and higher grew the towers of the mist, some rising to a level with the top of the farm hill — thin columns, transparent, moonlit, and showing through their beauty and ghostliness the one yellow light of a farm on the other side.

Nature has moods as well as forms and styles, and this was something in the eternally romantic. "But I had best cover the garden," I thought again. "There will surely be a frost."

FARM DIARY

My friend Paul Wilson gives me a chopping block such as I have long coveted for the farm. It is a strong, broad-based column of locust wood, and I can work at it comfortably without having to stoop over. / In a cornpatch by the road I come upon my neighbor Hudson Vannah and his helper Earl Baldwin, rooting up the rows of dead and withered plants and carrying away the stalks. The tractor suddenly backfires, and out of the pale field bursts a flock of blackbirds who take a grateful refuge in a nearby tree. A little later a grey squirrel passes us, running along the top of the boulder wall with a pale ear of corn held crosswise in his jaws. / A great basket of apples temporarily stored away in an unoccupied bedroom on

188

the cold side gives the interior of the farm a pleasantly autumnal fragrance. / The migrating waterfowl are coming in large numbers to the pond, and in the quiet of sunrise I often hear the popping of guns from duckblinds built on the shores of the shallow marshlands to the east of our bay. / Late in the afternoon with the sun scarce half an hour's distance above the pines, and I heard a truck coming towards the house; it is Lawrence with a fine load of white birch and yellow birch for the great fireplace. / Elizabeth likes to be read to while darning socks, and we have just begun an old novel of Maine.

The general term "Science" is very much with us these days, and I often find myself wondering if those who use it have much idea of what they mean. What is "Science" and more particularly, "a Science"? As I muse upon my own question, I am certain of one thing, to wit, that a share of our present troubles comes from our being led by the nose by a number of completely bogus sciences. Not all the king's horses would get me to name them! To my mind, however, the pretensions to being "sciences" now being put forward by certain departments of knowledge have just about as much authority as the pretensions of phrenology or the scrying of tea leaves. It is to be noted, moreover, that the use of the scientific method does not make a study a "science." My own definition? I stick to the hint given by Descartes — a science is a part of knowledge able at any time to consider its given realm and make with foreknowledge and certainty a prophecy concerning the working of its laws.

XXXIX

Four days of an almost southern warmth follow the first frost, and August resuming to September's landscape, visits the far horizons with a peaceful haze of smoky blue. By day thin clouds lie as seeming still as if they had been painted on the sky, and by night, and rather strangely, the northern lights tower above the warm earth and the placid air, the mysterious glowing centering on the zenith rather than about the pole. Some of us like the change and welcome the higher temperature recorded near the kitchen door, others of us — and I fear I am one of them — are made ungratefully uncomfortable, and working about, glance at the barn weathervane and hope it will presently swing into the north.

Grateful or ungrateful as we may be, the days are too fine to spend five minutes indoors, and I have used them working mornings in the kitchen garden and splitting wood in the afternoons. Some of the birch Lawrence brought me is in rather heavy "junks," and needs another session with chopping block and axe.

It has been a curiously windless summer, and these days, too, are very still. As I worked with the strawberries this morning in the growing silence and the mellow autumn light, now kneeling by the plants, now standing up and working with a light hoe, a thought came into my head of how good country smells can be and of how varied they are throughout the year. As I grubbed about close to the plants, hunting and pulling out any small, intrusive weeds, gone from the earth was the August smell of summer and dust and watered soil and watered leaves, gone the smell of earth which had a teeming earth life of its own. This September earth had lost warmth; it no longer dried out; in a few weeks it would be a cold and wintry mire with the cold smell of mire.

The seasons have their fragrance. In summer there is a smell of greenness, of heat, and grass and surface dust; in autumn the fragrance is one of cold dews and ripeness, of fallen leaves and the tang and ferment of leaves, of a world smouldering and withering away in the year's invisible fires. Sometimes the good hearty reek of some field crops is carried to the nose, and when an evening wind humid with a threat of rain blows through our kitchen windows a good, honest, country smell of cabbages. With winter will come a new earth and seasonal smell, fierce and keen and very real — the smell of snow.

What a world of the nose the country can be from the cidery smell of apples rotting in the brown, frosty grass under a wild apple tree to the honorable aroma of freshly dug onions spread on sacking in the autumn sun. There are plenty of others, hearty enough, some of them, but all, somehow or other, fit into a country world.

I meant to stay out of doors in the writing of these notes, but I find now that I must step inside if I am not to forget one of the most characteristic of good autumnal smells. Going to see friends yesterday on a small matter of farm business, I stepped into a kitchen which was all order and sunlight and the smell of cooking "piccalilli."

It was enough to make one lyrical, so completely blessed, so wholeheartedly good was that fragrance of spices and "garden sass" up-breathing from an enamel cauldron on the stove! The sunlight slanted on the linoleum floor, the family cat rubbed against my leg, and I stood there a moment lost — lost in a dream of boyhood and other kitchens, of another sunlight and unforgotten presences, and all the long and varied years.

FARM DIARY

Neighbors' Night at the Grange and three of our prettiest girls, dressed in costumes of the 80's from the family attics, sing an amusing, topical song. I can see that all three young ladies are taller than the original wearers of the rich, old-fashioned silks. / The telephone rings and our kind friend and next-door neighbor Louise Winchenbaugh

193

calls up to tell me that she is churning today, and would I like a pound of the fresh, unsalted butter? Indeed we would, and I shall stroll down for it early this afternoon. / Hardy crysanthemums now coming into bloom. / Elizabeth absent for the evening, having gone to Damariscotta to a ladies' party.

When I am here by myself, and the small dog and I share together the too-quiet evening and the open fire, I read the agricultural papers and journals which have been put aside in the kitchen cupboard for just such a solitary night. I never read through such a basketful without being struck by the good, sound, honest English of the writing, by the directness and simplicity of the narratives, and by the skill and forthright vigor of the arguments. Whether the topic be tomatoes or ten-penny nails, their writers know how to say things and say them well.

I am glad that the country world thus retains a power to use our English tongue. It is a part of its sense of reality, of its vocabulary of definite terms, and of its habit of earthly common sense. I find this country writing an excellent corrective of the urban vocabulary of abstractions and of the emotion disguised as thinking which abstractions and humbug have loosed upon the world. May there always be such things as a door, a milk pail, and a loaf of bread, and words to do them honor.

XL

The dark came early that night, and with it the wild, torrential rain of a "line storm" which had been moving up the coast. Lamplit and cheerful from within, the kitchen window panes looked out into a pitch blackness of wind and storm, and standing a moment by the open door, I could hear the unquiet stir of the nearer trees, and the great sound of rain falling everywhere in the immense and lonely dark.

Not a very good night for a church supper, yet not a night to keep the adventurous at home. Elizabeth brought in our old hats and oilskins. I lit the lantern we leave burning in the kitchen when we go forth of nights, and the rooms being one by one darkened, we climbed into the car and drove off in the rain. Streaming torrents lashed against the windshield and the clicking, energetically busy wipers, and at a turn of the road a surge of the gale drove through the windshield beam and the slanting, silvery rain a great, drenched gust of golden leaves.

"I wonder if many will come?" said Elizabeth from beside me in the darkness of the car. "They'll come," I answered, "but you'll find them arriving a bit late. Well, here we are."

We had ourselves come a little early, and there were but three or four cars standing outside the church when we drove up to the curb. On the street level, the old brick edifice was as dark as a tomb though one light shone very brightly over the entrance door; it was the church basement whose windows glowed with preparations and a sense of welcoming. Entering by a side door, we found ourselves in the big coat-room of the Sunday School, and reassured by a very genial, all pervading smell of a meat dinner.

A friendly hand in the kitchen waved to us a first welcome; it was Mrs. Tom Sherman working briskly with the other ladies of the congregation getting dinner ready. One could see the steam of potatoes, and a long table of plates, each garnished with a pale wedge of pie. Seated together on a Sunday School bench standing against a wall, Elizabeth and I watched the outside door open and swing back and the guests assemble, both of us looking for neighbors and friends amid the arriving crowd closing umbrellas and pulling off raincoats and rubbers. It was largely a grown-up gathering except for the pretty schoolgirls who acted as waitresses and the usual cornerful of boys with hair slicked back for the occasion above their fresh, out-of-door faces. The room which only a quarter of an hour before had been so empty was filling with a stir of people, and growing vocal with a cheerful, social noise of welcomes, greetings, and pleasant small-talk.

No one that I could see gave any signal, but presently we all stood up and began to move rather solemnly into the dining room. It was the Sunday School basement, and there was a raised platform at one end enthroning a very solemn ecclesiastical chair of American Gothic in some dark wood. When we had taken our places at long tables, the minister, our friend Rev. Cecil Witham asked a blessing I thought full of dignity, the stir in the kitchen quieting a moment as he spoke. Then in came the first plates, and with the first plates a new mood. Deft hands and a girl with a pretty smile suddenly appeared beside us, and placed steaming plates before us both. On each were hamburg cakes well done, plus a dishing of hamburg gravy, a mound of mashed potato, and a mound of mashed and buttered turnip. There was bread already on the table and extra butter. Again rather solemnly but very contentedly we all fell to.

More hands appeared from behind, hands holding huge white-enamel pitchers. "Will you have coffee?" "There's lots more hamburg; take all you want." "More gravy?" "Like some more turnip?" "Apple or mince?" "Anybody want seconds on pie?"

A good, substantial supper, we agreed, as we drove back to the farm. It was still pouring, the silver rods of driving rain slanting past the street lights on their poles above the road.

The last porcupine who came to eat the old "high top" apples made such a racket at midnight that the noise woke me out of a sound sleep. The creature squealed like a small, angry pig who had been refused permission to go to the party. / The hunting season begins, and in the profound, golden peace of the windless morning I hear a faraway hound give tongue and the occasional pop! of a gun from the deep woods. / A scurry in the wall, a gnawed apple on the kitchen floor, and my own hunting season opens. The restless, adventuring rat is in search of winter quarters, and we had our first invaders. Score: five in three nights and we are sure to have others. / Elizabeth buys the farm another hand woven blanket with a pattern of cheerful rainbow stripes from end to end. "Not one of my regular blankets," explains the genial weaver. "I made it up just to show what colors I could furnish, but you can have it now that the season is over." / The leaves fall, the wind blows, and the farm country slowly changes from its summer cottons into its winter wools.

I have lately been working with machines, and I venture to set down here something of my growing quarrel with one aspect of modern machinery. Again and again as I study these contrivances, I am struck by their increasingly dehumanized and even anti-human perversity of design. That a machine is both a machine and something meant to be used by a human being is apparently the last thing to be considered in the blueprints. Not only is one now confronted with some absurdity of design which makes repairs difficult, but also with absurdities of structure which make difficult and even dangerous the care of the machine necessary to its daily use. Among such deviltries — and they are numberless — are parts so placed that only a contortionist could reach them, spaces through which the hand must pass which are too small and cramped for the hand, and oil drains which require a gutter if the oil is not to mess up everything.

The country tradition of the handicrafts would be ashamed of any such neglect and scorn of our humanity. I am sure, moreover, that this same scorn and perversity has a role in the making of our fatigues and discontents. It may be a mere detail, but it's not a small one when you are tying yourself in exasperated knots with a greasy monkey wrench.

XLI

The blue Kennebec lay below us to the west, its rushing waters rippled with the sunlight of a bright October morning, and to the east and above us on hills and mountains, the forest blazed in its autumnal coat of many colors. Along these waters and through this same wilderness, I remembered, Arnold had made his way to Quebec at the beginning of the Revolution; over these very rapids his men had dragged their clumsy and heavily loaded *batteaux;* on these very slopes they had built their evening fires. In their village homespuns and cowhide boots, in their torn woolen stockings and woolen scarves, the figures of the expedition peopled the scene again in my mind's eye as I drove north, they, too, facing north in another splendor of autumn one hundred and seventy-one long years ago.

Uninhabited and for the most part uninhabitable, the forest still covers the lonely country of "the height of land" and the immense region of the boundary mountains. For well over a century lumber companies have used these hundreds of wilderness miles, and everywhere are old tote-roads leading to nowhere, their corduroy lengths and swamp crossings long ago sunk and rotted into the black forest mire. These last years bears have made it particularly their own, and a friend tells me that they are now so numerous that at the lumbercamps their prowling visits alarm newcomers from the French villages over the border.

And what shall one say of presences much more mysterious than bears? One of the "undeveloped townships" of the woods — or as we call them here, "plantations" — has from time immemorial borne the curious and lovely name of "The Enchanted." People may say to you of a neighbor, "He's gone hunting in The Enchanted." Fifty years ago in this plantation a wood voice, a seemingly human voice, sent a whole lumbercamp out searching in the night, yet in the morning there were no strange footsteps in the snow. Well . . . a Canada lynx can make very curious noises, but the old woodsmen always spoke of the sound they heard as "the voice," and the incident is remembered to this day.

With the cutting of so much spruce and pine, the forest is surely more of a hardwood region than it was in Arnold's day. On the tote-roads the pale and papery beech leaves now strew the forest clearings together with the deep scarlet of the maples and the beautiful tan-bronze of the fronded ash. Even so, the dark of the resuming evergreens is to be seen on every side, young pines, spruces, and fir balsams rising up in power from the floors of fallen leaves. On the

201

highways, too, pass thundering trucks piled with pine logs so giant that one wonders in what lost, hidden valley they were found.

At the village of The Forks, the expedition left the Kennebec and followed the Dead River to "the chain of ponds" and the ragged desolate, and stunted "height of land." What lumber there was seems to have been long ago appropriated, and vast fires have reduced the region to a wilderness of bush, bouldery mires, and alder-bordered ponds; much of it is now owned by a hunting and fishing club. I have had old woods-men tell me that in one of the ponds lies some waterlogged planking which some imagine is part of one of Arnold's *batteaux*.

I know the region, but last week I did not go beyond The Forks. The village today is but a line of rather frontierish houses built to the west of the confluence beyond an old-fashioned iron bridge painted an old-fashioned and faded red. The tourist season being about over, few cars overtook us driving on to Canada by the black road which crosses the boundary a good thirty miles east of Arnold's narrow ponds in their ar-chaic gully in the bush.

The old general store at The Forks, I noticed, stood closed and empty, though its black and gold sign was still fixed to the wall. There was something on it about fishing tackle, groceries, and cigars. A kind of porch stood before the door and the empty windows, and we sat down there awhile to rest ourselves from driving and listen to the murmur of the Kennebec below the bridge. The sounds of rivers can bemuse the mind, and I am sure that if I had but waited longer, I might have heard the far-off shouts of Arnold's men and the last of the talk and the voices as the expedition moved up the Dead River to the woods.

FARM DIARY

To Bingham, Maine, to give a lecture and to visit with our dear friend Arthur R. Macdougall, Jr., and his family. "Mak" is the author of the genial, amusing, friendly-spirited "Dud Dean" stories so cherished all over America by all good fly-fishermen. Moreover, he is a minister as well as a writer, and hearing that he was expecting guests, some youngsters of his congregation make him a present of partridges. So when Mrs. Macdougall calls us, Elizabeth and I sit down with the Emily to a wonderful dinner of partridge white-meat cooked to a turn and served with vegetables from the garden. / At a post office and country store in the mountains, am able to buy a new corn-popper, the first I have seen for years. / A pleasant, elderly woman who runs a tiny shop full of second-hand things and "antiques" tells Elizabeth that she was one of twenty-two children, all of whom lived. "We never took anything for sickness but Indian herb medicines. Father knew all the healing plants. He was wonderful." / At Waterville, a good shopping center, I succeed in getting myself a pair of shoes. This is triumph, for outside of my high winter boots and old work shoes, I am down to one rather battered pair with scuffed toecaps. / Returning to the farm late in the afternoon, find it coldish and empty of its usual sense of life, but this we presently overcome with a cup of strong tea and a great open fire.

Every autumn I watch for one great star. It is the star Capella, and when in September I look to the north and see it rising over the somber roof line of a deserted barn, I know that winter is near. Night after night it stands a little higher above the earth when twilight comes, and when arrives the true cold and the dark, it has cleared the floors of earth and the low mists and is rising on its great arc into that northeast whence come the birds whose clamor sometimes wakes us in the earlier night. There is an order established against whose laws only fools will struggle, an order whose acceptance is the very cornerstone of life and peace.

XLII

As I fell asleep, I could hear the rain lashing at the windows, and all the outer dark of the night beyond the lamplight and the walls was full of the noises of the storm. When I woke, a little before sunrise, I saw that it had cleared in the depth of the night, and that the gale from the North Atlantic had blown itself to rags like an old sail, leaving us a drenched earth and a tranquil and shining world. Looking toward the pond from the kitchen windows to the east, I could see the sun about to rise from behind a mere scarf of cloud which floated in bright air close above the ridge, and presently saw the cloud-edge gild itself with light, and the rim of the sun leap forth into the blue.

A new world came into being with the sudden gilding of that arc and sector of sunlight above the frail barrier of that last outpost of cloud. The hayfield slopes leaped into a new existence with the vast and sudden instancy of light, tree shadows sprang into being, and on the peaceful water of the pond, and to the south of the little island with its pines, there appeared a vast brilliance of mirrored and coldly-metallic light. Not only had the rain quieted the earth, giving it a moment of fixity and repose, but it had everywhere deepened the colors of the landscape, darkening the columns of the trees, and laying a hand of brightness on the fields.

The great water tank being at low ebb, I went down the eastern slope to the pump-house soon after I had built my morning fires. Halfway down to the pond is a cabbage patch belonging to my friend and neighbor Elwell Oliver, and the rain-washed plants glowed in the rain-washed air and against the autumn landscape like huge, rustic shapes of Chinese green-jade. I imagine the color was heightened, as well, by the bright darkness of a young and solitary pine I have allowed to grow up by a rock pile to one corner of the patch, for there it stood beyond the cabbage rows, the branches to the south thrust forth motionless into the increasing light of the morning sun.

The patch was alive with a migration of autumnal sparrows. It was a confusion of flying to and fro, of small, brownish birds, busy, restless, and searching for food, all in a restless sound of the small brushing by of feathers and the flutter of wings. There were a number of species, among them tree sparrows and fox sparrows, the latter predominating, both of these species being summer birds of the even higher north. I was particularly glad to see a single white-crowned sparrow foraging on his own. The birds perched upon the edges of the great cabbage leaves, which surprisingly did not bend with them; they inquired and searched about in a circle below the leaves; they flew to and fro between the patch and the small pine.

The coming of these northern sparrows down from Quebec and the frontiers of Ungava is a sign of winter. One of these cold nights we shall have snow.

FARM DIARY

The other night, just as I was putting the house to bed, I happened to remember that I had left a loaf of bread in the car, and stepped out into the pitch darkness to "fetch it in." Just as I reached the car and was feeling about in the darkness for the handle of the rear door, I heard some sizable animal stirring about quite near me, and a few seconds later the sound of the thing going toward the woods. By the time I had opened the car door and switched on the headlights, there was nothing whatever to be seen. A deer, perhaps, though deer are not much given to wandering about in pitch darkness. The car was standing on the farm lawn about fifty feet from the house. / Far down a hillslope and in all the golden quiet of the autumnal afternoon, I see a neighbor cleaning up his garden, and a pillar of bright flame burning in the center of the field. / The farm produce stands along Route 1 now come into their autumn glory of apples, squashes, and giant pumpkins backed by a shelf of cider jugs and jars of homemade "chili sauce." We stop at such a stand under a great, golden maple and Elizabeth buys some "cherry tomatoes" which turn out to be quite good.

Looking out over my fields, I think to myself that they not only have their own fierce American sun, but their own separate and American rhythm of time. I have long been convinced that one of the causes of dissension between Europe and America is a differing sense of time, the Europeans living by one sense of time, we by another. They live by the present and the past, we by the present and the future, and they live by a beat less mechanical than ours.

XLIII

There is a time in the later autumn when a vast cloud of fog forms almost every night above the pond, and, rising to fill the vale of the enclosing shores, spills over and out upon higher land as from a bowl filled and overflowing. No longer a vaporous mist but a mass thickened and opaque, it lies so dense at sunrise that sometimes I can scarce see from the farm to the farm gate, and I walk to whatever chores await me through a world without known bounds and suspended at once in morning silence and humid nothingness. Farmers, however, are early risers, and fog is a good carrier of sound, and presently I am sure to hear far noises across the texture of mist and perhaps the distant challenge of some farmyard chanticleer.

Thick as the fog lies floating on the earth, there is usually a blue sky standing open overhead. By ten o'clock, on any sunshiny morning, we commonly have our world again. The mist dissolves rather than lifts, and as it thins, the pasture fence and the golden trees appear, and the slow transformation scene ends with a view of the other side of the pond and its shore of pines scattered through with hardwoods in all their blazing color. Sometimes scarves and last wreaths of mist linger in the coldness of the shadowed woods, but the sun will have none of this, and presently these, too, melt and are gone, and the world belongs again to autumn and the blue and spacious day.

So peaceful it was this morning and so lovely, that I hurried through what indoor work lay ahead of me and turned again to out of doors. A delicate and scarcely perceptible haze of moisture remained in the air after the clearing, and it seemed to me that this residual transparency of mist gave an added glow to all the nearer scene. The maples, I noticed, were fast losing their foliage, and leaving the world to the leather-reds and russets of the oaks.

Halfway down the east slope, I could see my neighbors, the Olivers, gathering in their beans. The white horse Prince and the blue hayrack stood in the heart of the great field, and beyond the rack moved the figures of Father Oliver, his son Irving and four-year-old grandson John in a red sweater, bright as any autumnal leaf. The beans had been stacked on stout poles, as is our local custom, and from the house I could see Irving taking up, one after another, these brown and withered towers, first swaying the poles about and working them loose in the earth. Both Elwell and Irving then laid their huge burdens in the rack with the poles slanting forward, and each pole, I thought, seemed taller than a man.

No more would I look down and see these rustic pillars scattered over the field in the cold autumnal moonlight; no more would I see the small migrants flying to and fro between the pole tops and the ground. The load assembled, Irving climbed into the rack and took up the reins. Father Oliver then handed in the little boy and climbed in himself. The white horse started, stopped, and started again, and the load of harvest life came slowly up the hill.

The old-fashioned "baked bean" is an important part of our farm economy in this higher north. With plenty of "baking beans" in storage, a piece of salt pork, and a jug of molasses in the "buttery," a wood range that knows its business in the kitchen, and a family bean pot in the oven, we feel ready here for anything that may arrive when the north and east darken beyond the hills and a three day storm begins to howl.

FARM DIARY

Buy for ten cents at the rummage table of a Grange Fair a huge, old-fashioned, blue and white bandanna handkerchief of that older cotton which is softer and more pleasant to handle than modern cloth. Elizabeth thinks it has never seen use, and a relic of the 70's or 80's from some chest in a local attic. / Sundown, and a country road through the woods coming to an end with a somber arch of pines, and in the arch the bright sickle of the new moon unclouded and serene. / Shaken from the dooryard trees by a light, almost imperceptible wind, leaves drift down past the kitchen windows in the rhythm of the great flakes which so often announce the beginning of a night of snow. / Our friend Tom Sherman, standing firm-footed on the ridge pole of our barn, restores to its place and mounted on a new staff our "Johnny Ride the Sky," the horse-and-jockey weather vane which has come down to us from the farm's horse and buggy years.

How pleasant to spend some time with a singing family! During my own lifetime, one of the most dismal social changes of our world has been the disappearance of singing as part of human life and the work that has to be done. People used to sing, now you scarcely hear anyone even whistle. The world is poorer for the loss. There is nothing like music for giving one a sense of solidarity, and it lightens both labor and the heart.

XLIV

So comes to an end as pleasant an October as any of us can remember, an October so mild and warm that it might have been a second and more tranquil summer. Because there have been few heavy rains it has been a fine season for field work and harvesting, and on all the farms the autumn ploughing has been unhurriedly done, the potatoes dug, the apples picked, the field manured, and the house gardens raked clean of the pale and sprawling ghosts which the heavier frosts left withering on the ground. Now comes November and a colder sky with a prophecy of winter in its lessened and russet light, and something of the vast silence of winter in the air.

It is a time for rustic satisfaction, and a time, in the old phrase, "to count one's blessings," be they golden Hubbards or a barrel of farm cider, yet a touch of melancholy can steal its way into the mood. The great, earthy, and out of door tasks of the farm are over and done, and on these cold nights when a rising wind rattles to the windows and the ragged clouds sail across the moon, we know in our warm kitchens what will presently come down upon us from the solitudes of the north. Strengthened and provisioned like fortresses, our cordwood stacked under cover and our cellars filled, we should not fear the northeaster and the wind running in above the sea.

Fortresses we are, fortresses of the life of man in the beauty and glare and sunshine of the snow. In Maine we call our preparation for the siege — and the phrase is ancestral — "housing up." The women of the farms now put in order the rooms which will not be used, stripping the beds and folding up and laying away the blankets, placing chairs to one side, and carefully putting each thing that might be breakable into a bureau drawer. During the last of autumn, when such rooms are not too cold, these deserted chambers have a magnetic quality of attracting to their chilly emptiness all sorts of things which must be kept at a proper temperature, baskets of winter pears, for instance, and late-ripening apples, and even jars of jelly put aside to "set" awhile.

Today Elizabeth, together with our neighbor Mrs. Ruth Erskine (who is pianist at our Grange), has been busy at this domestic ritual. Blankets have been hanging on the line all morning in this coldish light, the hooked rugs have been laid flat and swept on the grey veranda, and the company tea cups taken from their shelf on the what-not in the parlor and put away, each wrapped in its bit of newspaper. The house retreats upon itself but its life is not weakened; it is merely given more unity and concentration.

It is the task of the men to see to the state of the house and barn, make repairs, and check on the primary supplies. If there is a coal stove in use part of the winter, the coal must be in; kerosene barrels filled, too, and the stove wood as far as possible got under cover. Today Ellis Simmons and I have been working outside. The screens have come off, some willingly, some obstinately, the storm doors and the double shutters fitted, two more cords of wood stacked, and the pond water-system drained and the great pump greased and laid up for winter.

A little after four o'clock a great wild sound in the sky sent us all rushing out of doors. A huge flock of Canada geese, flying unusually low, were passing by directly above the farm. Arriving from the east, the line swung south toward the local inlets and the sea, hovered for a few minutes in milling indecision, and disappeared, still apparently confused, into the cold and wintry light a little south of west.

FARM DIARY

Another community supper, this one given by the Nobleboro church and Grange together. The door of the Grange Hall stands open, a glare of electric light, and in the starlit darkness beyond, loom the vague shades of the farm trucks and autos which have brought in their people to the baked beans, brownbread, and pumpkin pie. / Have a grand talk with Linwood Palmer, Jr. / On the way home from supper, the car going rather slowly over the country road, a raccoon runs in the headlight beam for about thirty feet, and then turns off to the right into the roadside darkness and the underbrush. As he turns, he glances sideways at us, and we see the masklike coloration across the eyes. / About a mile from the farm, some beavers have dammed a culvert under the railroad track through which a vague brook joins the pond, and have raised the level of the backed-up water a good three feet. / A mild afternoon, and Elizabeth busy with a trowel naturalizing tiger-lily bulbs in various half-wild corners of the nearer land.

However various may be the tasks which man is given to attend to upon this earth, his major occupation is a concern with life. To accomplish this duty, he must honor life, even if he honors it but blindly, knowing that life has a sacredness and mystery which no destruction of the poetic spirit can diminish. The curtain has just rung down on a great show and carnival of death and the air is still poisoned and we are poisoned. Our strength and intelligence have been used to counter the very will and purpose of the earth. We had better begin considering not what our governments want but what the earth imposes.

XLV

Behind the panelled door with its yellow paint and old-fashioned iron latch, the farm and its guests have gone to bed, and I am staying up late to write in the kitchen by lamplight and the open fire. A bitterly cold northwest wind, which the coming of night has increased rather than subdued, is howling by outside, driving before it and across the moon a torn and immense floor of rushing cloud, and the whine and wintry cry of the high wind sounds for the first time this year about the house.

Our guests are a young lieutenant of Marines and his wife who were married only this summer, he the son of an old friend whom we watched grow up from a small boy to one of those tall young men who set the pattern of a tall generation. For years a fighter-pilot in the Pacific, he is now a "GI" student at a not-too-distant college, following some course he hopes will get him somewhere, and, like a boy again, taking his text books and manuals to class. To us, he is "Sonny," his family nickname, and his charming lady, to whom I have taken a particular liking, is Ethel. Earlier in the evening, I built a comfortable fire for them in their room on the upper floor, and now they have said "good night." Elizabeth too has taken her book and retired.

A mood coming over me to take a solitary walk, I have been out for a stroll under the high wind and the moon. The length of the road I followed leads like a cart track through the level land of our own higher fields, having our pasture woods to one side, and to the other the farm itself, with a wide glimpse of the slopes below it and the pond. Overhead streamed the great earth ceiling of broken shapes, and torn islands and huge continents of vapor, now dimming and obscuring a moon almost at the full, now surrounding it with an opalescence and a bronzy and dissolving glow, with a wild halo at once vaporous and metallic and full of the vast torment and rushing of the air.

Beneath this sky and its wilderness of everchanging, darkening, and reappearing light, the chilled earth lay leafless and open to the onslaught of the wind. The new grass of the earlier autumn, already blanched by the frosts, though seeming at first almost without motion, was nevertheless wanly astir, trembling a little and lifelessly on the road's edge; the pines beyond tossing their higher branches and filling the moonlit air and the shrieking wind with the thin undertone of a green, incessant sigh. From the red oaks, which had kept some of their leaves, came another sound, a wild, dry, and melancholy shrilling, and every now and then I could see the huge oak leaves in the lower air, blowing down the wind in furious gyrations soon hidden by a dimming of the moon.

Now it is the farm again, the quiet table, and the fire. Not only is the small dog asleep in his basket, but I take it that sleep fills the whole house, for there is not a ghost of sound. Only the wind is awake, and even as I write these lines, I can hear a gust of leaves from the lawn blown with a kind of fierce whisper against the wall.

FARM DIARY

Two wood fires, one in the kitchen range, one in the great fireplace, burn all day long, and smoulder away to nothing in the night. The stove in the center of the house, however, now using coal, keeps a steady core of comfortable warmth in the heart of our winter fortress. / Our neighbor Mildred Ricker comes over to help us put up some jars of winter pears. / First ice in the rainbarrel, and no mere glaze but a solid lid about two inches thick, a night of bitter cold having begun before sundown at the cheerless close of a cheerless day. / Contrasted with the sounds of animal unrest one hears from the woods at night in spring, the farm woods of early winter seem strangely silent. Looking towards them from the house door on a moonlit night, I hear only silence itself across the silent fields. / When I face a winterish day warmly dressed from high boots to woolen cap, the woolen clothes give me a sense of protection and stout well-being. Yesterday, looking at my cotton overalls hanging in the washroom, I wondered when such things were worn and why.

At a little concert in a country hall, there is singing by a young people's choir and a number of what we call here "instrumental selections." Presently a woman of middle age whom I have never heard before rises and sings beautifully a lovely song of the great Elizabethan heritage, and there comes over me a sense of the poignancy and dignity to which the human spirit can rise, and I realize again that one of the great functions of any art is the constantly renewed revelation of the possible greatness of the human spirit.

XLVI

As the seasonal light decreases, and the arc of our northern sun becomes a mere geometric leftover of its midsummer sweep and exaltation, I watch the pond changing color from its autumnal blue to a kind of austere and silvery grey. Now that the water is becoming almost as cold as the air, the great fog-bank which used to gather on frosty nights is to be seen no more, though once or twice, after a night of bitter cold, I have seen vague wisps and thin tatters of trailing mist clearing off as the sun rose to begin his short-lived day. The other morning all the slopes were covered with frost, and the residual mists floated up the sides of the hills, and dissolved on the higher land into nothingness and light.

I have long had the notion that our northern ponds were at their bluest about a fortnight after the Vernal and, later, the Autumnal Equinox. The blue of early April, moreover, has always seemed to me brighter and more living than the colder and more severe blue of the clearer October air. In the full solar splendor of midsummer there is too much light in the sky to give us the blue of water at its best, and the pleasant, varied tones of summer are paler tones of the air and the mystery overhead. Now there has come a second paling and a second withdrawal, and though there is blue to be seen on the water, it is a blue which is near to silver and to steel. A force of nature itself, the pond awaits the deeper cold and its own emergence from some first and iron night floored with a first darkness and motionlessness of ice. The trees of the shore are skeletons of winter, the grasses and sedges of the little beach have withered to spears of straw and russet brown, and on the tiny crescent of cold sand a submerged garland of matted oak-leaves checks the ripples blown ahead of a morning wind which has risen with the sun.

FARM DIARY

Deer-hunting season ends, to the relief and satisfaction of the farm. It is pleasant to think that we shall hear no more shots from the woods. / The state takes over a short length of our town road which is almost impassable in winter, sends us a junior steam-shovel and a state engineer, and our younger neighbors build the new length under the direction of our own village "road commissioner." The job seems to be going on as a sort of working holiday, and the weather has been pleasant the whole week. A very busy and sociable scene. / Little John Oliver's fourth birthday, and well do I remember his arrival! He came on a wintry morning of cloud-covered skies and a searching wind, and as Elizabeth and I walked down to the Olivers', the cold wintry air was being continuously shaken by the distant and heavy thunders and rolling detonations of the firing from the forts along the coast. / I open the storm door and gaze out into the night. It is pitch dark and utterly silent, and past the streaming lamplight falls the snow.

So draws to a close the country year. It is late at night, and musing here alone in the kitchen of the farm, my papers and pencils spread about on the table under the peaceful light, I venture to set down a statement of a country man's unchanged belief. What has come over our age is an alienation from Nature unexampled in human history. It has cost us our sense of reality and all but cost us our humanity. With the passing of a relation to Nature worthy both of Nature and the human spirit, with the slow burning down of the poetic sense together with the noble sense of religious reverence to which it is allied, man has almost ceased to be man. Torn from earth and unaware, having neither the inheritance and awareness of man nor the other sureness and integrity of the animal, we have become vagrants in space, desperate for the meaninglessness which has closed about us. True humanity is no inherent and abstract right but an achievement, and only through the fullness of human experi-

223

ence may we be as one with all who have been and all who are yet to be, sharers and brethren and partakers of the mystery of living, reaching to the full of human peace and the full of human joy.